QUIET WATERS
OF
INSPIRATION

IN VERSE

Poetic inspiration for much of life
By: LaDean McGonigle

Published By
LaDean McGonigle

Copyright © November 1996
LaDean McGonigle

All scripture verses are taken from the King James Version of the
Holy Bible.

First edition
First Printing - 1,000 - December 1996

Cover photograph is of Merritt Dam in the heart of the Nebraska
Sandhills at Valentine, NE

Additional copies are available. For your convenience, an
order form can be found at the back of this book.

ISBN 1-57502-384-9

Printed in the USA by

M ORRIS
PUBLISHING

3212 E. Hwy 30
Kearney, NE 68847
800-650-7888

I would like to dedicate this book to my husband, Dale, who never complained, even when I stayed in my office sometimes when he was home from the truck. To my whole family for their support and to my dear friend, Janice, for being more inspiration than she knows.

I also want to thank my friends, Sherry, Linda and Lee for being my sounding boards and critics.

I want to let my special friend, Vada, know it means a lot to me to see her eyes light up when I give her a new writing of mine to read. Friends are indeed special, one and all.

Thank You Dad for your poem "Grandpa's Teeth". I'm sure people will enjoy it.

I, LaDean (Blauvelt) McGonigle, was raised in the Sandhill area of Nebraska at Thedford. I spent most of my young life there, leaving only after graduating from high school. I moved to the city of Lincoln. I attended church in Milford with my cousin Marilyn and met my future husband, Dale.

We stayed mostly in the Milford, Friend, Beaver Crossing area these more than thirty-seven years and raised our family here. I return to the Sandhills to go fishing and visit my family, enjoying every moment I am there.

We worked in farm construction side by side, including our children, for many years. When I retired for medical reasons in 1983, Dale went into trucking. When he was hurt severely in a truck accident more than five years ago, I took care of him at home. I asked the Lord to give me something to do at home to keep me sane, something that I would enjoy and something that would make us a living. He gave me poetry. I had never written before, but I can say with all sincerity that I enjoy it. It has kept me sane but the last part is for future reference.

Dale went back to trucking after several months. God is so good.

May the Lord bless you in the reading of this book as he has blessed me in the writing. Enjoy!

John 4:13-14

"*Jesus answered and said unto her, Whosoever drinketh of this water shall thirst again: But whosoever drinketh of the water that I shall give him shall never thirst; but the water that I shall give him shall be in him a well of water springing up into everlasting life.*"

Friendship
and
Love

John 15:13

"Greater love hath no man than this, that a man lay down his life for his friends."

Friendship is: a gift from God. It is a two, or more part gift given to two, or more people to be treasured and handled with care. When the gift is not properly taken care of by all parties involved the gift loses it's meaning and may become useless. It cannot be set aside, laid away, put on a shelf, ignored, misused, or taken for granted. Should any of these occur, hurt, or misunderstandings come to be causing the gift great damage. These must be righted as soon as possible so as to restore the gift to its original luster.

Should the gift be rejected after a trial period by either party, or by lack of commitment, it may have to be returned to God. This does not mean that it was not meant to be. It only means that everyone has been given a free choice by God. One may not be at the place in their relationship with him to accept such a precious gift.

Sometimes one does not know how to accept such a gift. Some do not know the meaning of friendship and even with help are not willing to learn. Other times self-centeredness, or more commonly called selfishness, prevails creating the lack of an open heart.

God understands. He will open another even more wonderful door to friendship which will, through him, bring a blessing more than you can measure.

Place your trust in him and though you may find disappointment for a moment, the long range benefits are more wonderful than you can imagine.

Look deep into your heart to see what loving treasures you may have overlooked. God can magnify, and restore to you his very best.

Exodus 33:11a "*And the Lord spake unto Moses face to face, as a man speaketh unto his friend.*"

Proverbs 27:6a "*Faithful are the wounds of a friend.*" *v.10a* "*Thine own friend, and thy fathers friend, forsake not.*"

May God Bless You in your friendship today, as He has blessed me. Special Friends are God's gift to us. Let us treasure them.

Dedicated to my special friend, Janice

Dear Friend

Dear Friend, you mean the world to me,
your friendship is such a treasure.
No matter what we seem to do,
it is such a pleasure
to see you smile, or hear you laugh,
or know that you are there
to listen and to hear me out,
no matter what I share.
Or be the nice distraction
when things have got me down,
it really tends to ease my mind
just to know that you're around.

This world would be a better place
if more people were to be,
the kind that you can count on,
like the friend you are to me.

Good Friends

Good friends are sometimes hard to find,
someone to share your heart and mind,
share what's down inside your soul,
be there when needed to console,
to hold your hand when things get rough,
to make you laugh when things are tough.

Good friends are a special breed,
they lift you up when you're in need,
they enjoy your company a lot,
they never put you on the spot,
they intercede in prayer for you,
they take your hand and show they're true.

Good friends are good for you,
they reciprocate, they lean on you,
they make you know you're alive,
they need your love, they make you thrive,
they like to see your smiling face,
you for each other have a place.

Good friends respect each others space,
but they're not selfish, they share with grace
time and talent, one on one,
side by side having fun
with each other for a time,
without reason, without rhyme.

Friendship is a two-way street,
it's where two people agree to meet
on common ground where neither's best,
but set apart from all the rest,
for hearts in confidence agree
that I'm for you and you're for me.

You're
Just A Thought Away

When the day is such a pretty day and the birds are full of song,
my heart is full of happiness with nothing to go wrong,
I feel the need to share the things that have happened in this day;
alas, there's no-one else around, but you're just a thought away.

There are the times I'm all alone or times I'm just too busy
to have the fellowship I crave or when I'm in a tizzy
with all the things ahead of me and no time left to play;
then's the time I need you most and you're just a thought away.

I'm thankful for the times we have when we can be together,
for it fills the heart with needed joy, makes cares light as a feather.
Then however time comes and goes, or what distance
between us lays,
there will never be real loneliness, for you're just a thought away.

My Special Friend

Like the bird's first song in the early morn at the
breaking of the dawn,
or when the rainbow comes at the end of a storm
with the sun when the clouds are gone,
is the cheer that's sent to a weary heart at the
end of a trying day,
when words, in kindness, are given out by a friend
in a special way.

Just as a candle lights a darkened path when there's
need to find the way,
or a prism sends forth colors bright in a
wonderful display,
is the joy that abounds to one in need, who's spirits
are very low,
when a smile is given by a special friend that sets
the heart aglow.

As a fireplace sends out welcome warmth when
there's frost upon the ground,
or an ice-cold drink cools the thirsting tongue
when the summer is around,
so is comfort found in the presence now, of one
who is so dear,
as you are to me my special friend; thank you
for being here.

What Is Real

Real is what is actual, natural,
how it was made to be,
things in life we cannot change,
like what is real in you and me.
Self image is somewhat neglectful
when a reality check is made,
for it is exceedingly one sided
and just cannot make the grade.
The mirror is never truthful
when ourselves we look to see;
it is cold and flat and hard,
just a reflection of what might be.
We cannot see ourselves
in the way that others do,
they see life and warmth and vibrance,
the part of us that's true.
If we are loved and cared for
it gives reality quite a boost,
it will not let self indulgence
take a seat, or go to roost,
because we then return that love
letting self take second place
giving room to what is real,
filling us with grace.
If to see we must what we really are,
what we in truthfulness attend,
we must see ourselves as others do,
through the eyes and heart of a friend.

Friendship

(To my Valentine)

We see the beauty of the sunrise, the sunset paints the sky,
but in our hearts we know it's an illusion to our eye,
for the sun stands forever in it's place and we for a time do see
as the earth will circle onward because God said it would be.
Time goes on forever till it becomes eternity,
things are set in order, God gave us that guarantee.

A longing in the heart for friendship he in each gave a place
so we would feel for others and love we would embrace.
Although he himself our spirit fills, our human hearts
need our own kind;
a friend to love and care for is within his will designed.
He gave us ones within the home to be close to night and day,
but the need to grow with others for us he made a way.
When we let him choose for us the one to fit our need the best
we can rest assured that through his love we will both be blessed.

My friend you are the very one that he chose for me,
I want to tell you on this day set aside for love you have
been the key
to open up a part of my life closed to the world around,
so I could learn more of love and not in self be bound.
Thank You friend for letting me share part of me with you;
God will bless you for he knows just what love will do.

*"Love and your world is filled with sunshine;
Be to yourself and you're all alone."*

Friendships Past

As if carried on the winds of time
past friendships blow away,
to leave the heart with fond memories
to store against decay.
From time to time the breezes raise
to lift them and renew
the thoughts that bring again to life
things meant for only you.
You sift through them with beating breast,
recalling all that's fine,
then lay them gently down again
to hold till another time.
Sometimes the memories that come
bring loneliness and pain,
for things that you feel could have been
and things you want again.
You don't know what God had in mind
when you went your separate ways,
but you know that in His perfect plan
His compassion He displays,
for though you do not know ahead
what He has in store for you,
you know that you must wholly trust,
let Him do what He must do.
The time may come again sometime,
when in His wisdom He sees fit
to give the friendship back to you,
refined for your benefit.
Lord we realize this fleeting life
you hold within your hand,
whatever path for us you set, we'll try to understand.
If things don't end the way we'd choose,
we know You have command.
Thank You Lord for what You've done
and things ahead You've planned.

1 John 4:7

"Beloved, let us love one another, for love is of God.   And everyone that loveth is born of God, and knoweth God."

vs. 11-12

"Beloved, if God so loved us, we ought also to love one another.   No man hath seen God at any time.   If we love one another, God dwelleth in us, and his love is perfected in us."

Real Love

Real love is often thought to be
the feeling that you have
when things are really going great,
and nothing makes you sad,
like a new born baby in your arms,
new married's coming down the aisle,
a sweetheart in the bright moonlight,
or the glow of your best friends smile.

But real love comes through the test of time,
the sharing day by day,
honoring others above yourself
in a sincere, and heartfelt way;
taking time for caring, being faithful,
come what may,
encouraging, and being cheerful
though you may not feel that way;
loving your neighbor as yourself,
being patient, as well as kind,
giving help, and warmth to others
keeping always in your mind,
real love is never harmful,
and when you give your best,
others will receive a blessing,
and by God you will be blessed.

Rose Garden Of Love

A rose filled garden of love, found in the heart of a friend,
indescribable blooms of care and concern
ready to pluck and send
to someone in need of warmth, as a ray of sun to the soul,
extended in a hand of friendship, to mend,
to heal, to make whole.
A lovely rose covered with dewdrops of tears
may be shared with a broken heart,
or one with a velvety petal of peace, a calmness to impart.
Colorful roses of wisdom, a bouquet of great prize,
can be given with much kindness when the need should arise.
A rose of joy and thanksgiving may be given
when hope is high,
or one opened in full blown beauty when
there is a need to try.
A rosebud of promise may be given to
a new friend along the way,
as a recognition that more will come as it
matures day by day.
Wild roses spread along the way so those following behind
will see beauty and simplicity of friendship
in the love-path that's been outlined.
The rose fragrance of love will surround
ones that are far apart,
so memories of friends not forgotten will
stay near to the heart.
Roses for every occasion, every kind, shade, and size,
roses of friendship not taken for granted,
a goal to be realized.
The rose garden of love is a beauty,
friendship for every day,
God blessed for all situations and enjoyed in every way.

14

Love's Secret

There was a time that loneliness
found a place within my heart,
I did not know just what to do,
so I found a place to start.
I found and gave some of my love
to someone all alone;
I did not have too much to give,
as I had kept it as my own.
A funny thing did happen,
when I checked, I began to see
the loneliness was leaving
and there was still love left in me.
I thought I'd go still further
to see what happened then,
I proceeded to go out again
and make another friend.
The loneliness then vanished
and I found within my heart
that love had somehow blossomed
to become a lasting part.
Another thing then happened
when I began to share,
more love just kept coming,
with a whole lot more to spare.
I know I've found the secret
of what it means to love.
Love is really boundless;
I see God smiling up above.

*"Many waters cannot quench love, neither can the floods
drown it." Song of Solomon 8:7a*

Love

Love is not from the thoughts we have
after watching most scenes on T.V.,
they are thoughtless, mindless, immoral, set in sin,
things we shouldn't see.
Love is not as is portrayed within the ads
of the news stand magazine,
love is a wonderful gift from God sent to fill our very being.
It's a gift we give to others, it comes from within our heart,
it's warm and soft and caring, of ourselves we give a part.
It's when we hold that little child, or give Mom and Dad a hug,
it's when we take our spouse's hand and it gives our heart a tug.
it's when the smile of our dearest friend
inspires us to reach out and touch
them with a feeling deep inside that we love them very much.
It's not to be taken lightly for it reveals our inner self,
it will burst forth in the smile we give,
it's not something we put on a shelf.
We cannot wrap it and hide it, it would become stale and die,
it has to be daily given out with praise, or as coffee and pie.
It may be given out shyly, or it may come out in a rush,
but it fills us more as we use it,
it to us is luxurious and plush.
Sometimes we may feel empty, we feel we have to use a facade,
there is a deep void within ourselves
that can only be filled by God.
He fills us to the very brim with love, then we can to others give,
loving others as we do ourselves is the only true way to live.
Love is desired by all who live, it's a God given need we fulfill,
without it we will dry up inside and lack of it our insides kill.
Always reach out to others, we need of ourselves to give,
we live to give of our love to others so we ourselves might live.

Children and Families

What is more precious in our lives than the coming of a little child? God can bless our hearts in a special way with one of His little treasures. We only have to be open and receptive to His will in all situations. His guidebook, the Bible, can give us the instruction we need to care for His little one.

There are many places we can find His wisdom but the Proverbs will give us help in our own lives as well as the lives of the our children. To bless you soul read them over and over again.

Proverbs 22:6 "Train up a child in the way he should go, and when he is old he will not depart from it.

God's Little Treasure

There has entered into your lives now
a treasure from God above,
a precious little person
made for you to love.
God gave this one into your care
to teach and raise for right,
to watch over and protect
be it daytime or at night.
In turn this tiny little child
will fill your heart with joy
and individual talents
will preconceived ideas destroy.
For this is the one and only one
God make to be this way,
this is His personal gift to you
and it is up to you to pray
for God's guidance and His perfect will
as this little life you mold;
when you set a good example
God will His treasures to you unfold.

Precious memories as we go from one generation to the next. Traits passed on that warm the heart. High energy abounds that make me remember that I'm a grandma.

Thank You Lord for this little life. Maintain it with tenderness as you see fit.

My Love

Just a little towhead,
  big blue eyes I see,
  curls ringed all around,
  that's the one for me.

Smile upon the tiny face,
  crackers here and there,
  like to stole my heart away,
  that's my child so fair.

Little arms go 'round my neck,
  a sloppy kiss or two,
  makes me feel important,
  more than anything I do.

Sparkle in the pretty eyes,
  feet go everywhere,
  precious little toddler,
  God make me aware
  of all these lovely moments
  so they don't pass me by.
  Lord I love this little one,
  look down from on high.

Sleep has come upon the scene,
  peace all around to reign,
  sweet dreams come so gently,
  new found energy to gain.

Children are poetry in motion. We were watching our little ones play outside in the country. The smallest had never enjoyed the country life as yet. All the energy that was put out was a miracle of God. Making memories was what the day was all about.

If we take the time to enjoy what the Lord has given us and see things as the children do, then life will have more of a meaning to us.

We will go to bed tired, but happy with our lives.

This Little Child

Fuzzy, footed "jammies", sleepy little eyes,

had a long and busy day beginning near sunrise.

Helping Mommy bake a cake, giving Dad a little hand,

rolling in the lawn grass, playing in the sand.

Took some time to roller-skate with the neighbor kid,

smiled, laughed, had great fun in everything they did.

Didn't have time for a nap, would have taken

time from play,

the busyness has now taken toll, now it's time to pay.

Bath time transformed telltale signs of

all that has transpired,

the sweetness is the part that's left of the one that's tired.

Time to hear a Bible story, kneel to say the prayer,

dreamland is not far away, tucked in with teddy-bear.

Lord you know this little one means the world to me,

watch and protect throughout the night

till morning light we see.

Then guide each one as the day to us again you lend,

so we may raise this child the way you choose

as you your blessings send.

Our most priceless possessions in the natural are our children. The most serious side of us must come into play when we talk about their lives and their future.

It only makes sense to place them in the safe keeping of the Lord. Their very lives depend on it.

Our Children

God placed children in our lives, a gift He from heaven sends,
to enjoy, to raise, to dote on, their lives to us He lends.
We love, we feed, we bathe them, we let them play and have fun,
we send them to school, provide for their needs,
protect them sun to sun.
We help them with their homework, we teach them
garbage detail,
we teach them responsibility, hoping we don't fail.
We feel we're being good parents, we send them
to Sunday School,
but what is our example to them, what should be our rule?
Our God given responsibility is not just doing what others do,
it's going a little bit farther, it's to give them another view.
We should teach them from the Bible, practice what we preach,
lead in family worship, their young souls for Christ to reach.
We should go with them every Sunday to the Sunday School,
teach them Bible verses as we would in homework
from their school.
Expect them to live a lifestyle designed for us by God,
make it an everyday habit so we won't have to prod.
Leave them a rich inheritance, a gift of quality time,
spent in the luxury of love, then everything will turn out fine.
Be in tune with each other, share from what's in our heart,
this time won't be forgotten, in them we'll become a part.
God will bless our efforts in raising them for the Lord,
we will be bound together in love's unbreakable cord.
When these obligations, through us in God have been met,
we'll find this kind of living will never bring us regret.

God's Child

A tiny little child, never to know the light of day,
lost to us within the womb, God provided the way.
Broken hearts of the parents, Grandparents are feeling it to,
but God called it home before us, before it's precious
life we knew.
We must go on as always, initial grief will pass away,
God is so understanding, he knew it should be this way.
We'll never know the reason, but God is in control,
we gave him this life in the beginning and now he will console.
We have more to look forward to in Glory when we go
to be with the Lord
for we have ones of our family before us, ones we
would have adored.
We're not alone in this situation, many have traveled
this road before,
God's little angels are waiting for us to meet on that distant shore.
Thank You Lord for your kindness in protecting our
children this way,
we don't know what problems we'd be facing, what in our
path would lay.
You'll give us no more than we can handle, we must
remember that's in your word,
you've given us a blessing, on us your love you've conferred.
Mend our hearts now we're asking, we pray
for parents every where,
lead us to others that need us as our hearts you will prepare.
We look forward to doing your bidding, experience is hard
but it does work,
we are now even more tender, whatever calls we won't shirk.
You gave your Son so you know what we're feeling,
you never leave us alone,
now bless all the children around us, your love
to ours you've shown.

A Parent

What an awesome responsibility one begins to feel
when they become a parent, a new world to reveal.
The loving care that's needed in bringing up a child,
to a parent is a challenge, whatever temperament is styled.
As each child grows older, no matter what the age,
a parent still feels responsible through every growing stage.
Though taught the ten commandments, with good examples set,
a child still makes the choices that make a parent fret.
The parent begins to realize why their parents show concern
about the things they're doing, what they yet will learn.

Teach a child what's right and wrong, give them to the Lord,
He will take good care of them, your faithfulness He'll reward.
Show them that God's "rule of thumb" is always do your best,
to "love your neighbor as yourself" then He will do the rest.
In tenderness He'll keep them when on Him they do rely,
He'll always be there for them listening ever to their cry.

When Christ is shown in discipline and His Spirit when concerned
while bringing up the child, respect for parents will be earned.
Many pleasant memories will be made along the way
when loving care and kindness are shown from day to day.
Being a parent isn't easy, it takes concentrated prayer,
but God is at your alter, He will always meet you there.

Isaiah 40:11 "He shall feed his flock like a shepherd: he shall gather the lambs with his arm, and carry them in his bosom."

Special Days

A Mom

A Mom is a heart of love,
two arms that hold a child,
tenderness personified,
in goodness she is styled.
Warmth and comfort, so sweet and nice,
strength and gentleness, too,
all go into making a Mom
from anyone's point of view.
God made Moms so special,
each one by His divine will,
some come by it naturally,
some God's special plan to fulfill.
To guide a child to a fulfilling life
takes a God given talent,
much time devoted to the young,
wills and desires to confront.
Thought goes into what's best for them,
a plan for each is made,
as each one is so different,
they into new territory must wade.
They see in the child a picture of self,
things they might like to change,
but seeing what's best from God's point of view
must priorities rearrange.
Being a Mom may be hard to do,
it's a life full of sacrifice,
but when holding that precious little one,
anything is worth the price.
When little arms go around the neck,
the first time the word Mom is spoken,
when the little one snuggles against the breast,
the Mom's heart is broken
in thankfulness for this wonderful way of life
God has chosen to her to give,
and even though things may get a little tough,
there's no other way to live.

Isaiah 66:13a "As one whom his mother comforteth, so will I comfort you."

My Father's Love

My Father is the greatest guy,
he's always been my friend.
An upright citizen I've become,
guided by my Father's hand.
He taught me responsibility,
and how to take a stand
for right, no matter what it takes;
he's a good, and upright man.
He taught me there's good in all of us,
that everyone is my neighbor.
He told me there's beauty in everything,
our God above has created.
He has shown me the way to show kindness,
he has shown me the way to show love,
he has set me a good example
in everything that he does.

I know that as I grow older,
I realize more every day,
God gave me a wonderful Father;
he's the greatest in every way.

Proverbs 22:6 "Train a child in the way he should go, and when he is old he will not depart from it."
Ephesians 6:1-3 "Children, obey your parents in the Lord, for this is right. Honor thy father and mother--which is the first commandment with a promise--that it may be well with thee and that thou mayest live long on the earth."

The First Easter

The Sabbath day had ended, the sun would rise again,
the women began approaching the tomb of their dead friend.
He had been beaten so severely, then hanged upon a cross,
they'd buried him securely, suffering a great loss.
They planned to place upon him spices showing their great love,
but much to their amazement, there sat an angel from above.
The great stone was rolled away, his body was no more,
they wondered what had happened to this friend they did adore.
Then they began remembering what friend Jesus to them had said,
that after time within the grave he would raise up from the dead.
They began rejoicing, they ran to tell their friends,
"Friend Jesus now has risen," credence to his life would lend.

We now have this same savior, all others we must tell,
the same news that was given that we now know so well.
For our loved ones we are praying, to our neighbors
show his love,
so we together will be joined with Jesus in heaven above.

Read: Matthew, chapters 27 and 28.
Luke, chapters 23 and 24.

These at the sight to the tomb had previously been told many awesome things. As we read the scriptures we can see it all.

To those at that time it was just their friend. They were grieving a friends loss. I wonder how much attention they had paid to what he had previously told them. It had not really reached their hearts until they saw that he had indeed risen from the dead.

They were as we. We hear, we know, but it takes a bit longer for reality to come to us. I think it is the syndrome of "we have to see to believe". Lord help our unbelief.

Christ Rose Again

We read about Christ's birth and celebrate on Christmas day,
we talk about His life and how he lived from day to day.
We speak about the miracles He performed without mistake,
we remember His last supper when we of communion partake.
We see that through His life He lived without a sin,
but what if after all of this, He hadn't rose again?

We know about the love He gave to all within His path,
we've heard about the temple and the merchants
incurring His wrath.
We see what was accomplished with the twelve disciples
He did teach,
we know that little children were His love and we are to reach.
We feel the devil got his due when he tempted Christ to sin,
but what if after all of this he hadn't rose again?

We tell about the woman He forgave while at the well,
we speak about the rich young man Christ told
"Go; your holdings sell."
We talk about friend Lazarus He raised up from the dead,
we read that on His last day He was beaten till He bled.
We know He hung upon a cross, He died for us and then,
Praise God! after all of this, He did, HE ROSE AGAIN!!

Thanks

Our forefathers had their Thanksgiving
with Indian folks that they knew,
thanking God for His many Blessings
and for friend's help in making it through
the winter, the summer and harvest,
for planting and hunting for food,
for help in their many endeavors,
with starting in this land anew.

With us it's become a tradition;
do you remember the reason why?
Do we give God thanks for our blessings,
or just gather for turkey and pie?

Let's take time and think of the good things
God has done for us this year.
Let's thank Him and be grateful
for family and friends we hold dear.

Lord, we thank you for the privilege
of living in this land we love
and pray for continued blessings
that flow down to us from above.

1 Thessalonians 5:16-18
"Rejoice Evermore.
Pray without ceasing.
In everything give thanks: for this is the will of God in
Christ Jesus concerning you."

What Am I Thankful For?

If someone were to ask me what I was thankful for today,
I'd have to tell them of the many things God has sent my way.
I'd tell them of the paintbrush that he'd used to paint the sky,
of the rays of sun that touched me so I'd know
he was standing by.
Then I'd tell them of the joy that fills my heart and soul
because he knows the cares I have and sends them to console.
I'd also have to tell them of what he's whispered in my ear,
so I'll be looking forward to the changes that will appear
when I stand aside and let him work his wonders in the heart
of the ones I care and pray for knowing he will do his part.
Then I'd tell them there were little things in my living day to day,
that come to hurt or confuse me if let them go their way,
but he reaches down when I least expect and with his gentle touch
smooths them out and lets me know he loves me so very much.
I'd tell them things aren't always perfect for I get in the way
of what he'd like to do for me, because I want my say,
but when I see what could have been had I just let go,
he forgives and we start anew because he loves me so.
Remind yourself daily of the things God does for you
so if you're asked you'll be sure to know and you can
tell them too.

"Thou hast turned for me my mourning into dancing: thou hast put off my sackcloth, and girded me with gladness; to the end that my glory may sing praise to thee, and not be silent. O Lord my God, I will give thanks unto thee for ever." Psalm 30: 11&12

34

A Celebration

We're celebrating the Christ of Christmas,
the birth of a little child,
God's Son in the form of mankind,
so pure and undefiled.
He was laid in a common manger
with animals sharing the hay,
His coming was plain and simple,
for God had planned it that way.
He came here to walk with the humble,
He came to sit with the poor,
He came and talked with the learned,
He's the king man was looking for.
He came to bring us a message,
repent and leave all your sin.
He then gave his life to redeem us,
so we could a new life begin.
He's coming again in the heavens,
His face and glory we'll see;
so don't forget your Christ this Christmas,
celebrate his love with me.

"For God so loved the world that he gave His only begotten Son, that whosoever believeth in Him should not perish but have everlasting life." John 3:16

Christmas Thoughts

A friend asked me the other day,
"Is your Christmas shopping done?
Have you decorated your Christmas tree?
Is Christmas Baking fun?
Are you planning for a great big feast,
or going to see your Mother?
Have you seen the pretty Christmas lights?
Don't you think Christmas is a bother?"

It made me stop and think awhile,
to ponder in my heart;
what things mean the most to me,
in what things do I take part?

Then there came the still small voice,
to remind me of our Savior,
how he came to earth as a little child,
and the reason that he was here for.
He came to live within our hearts,
to be with us every day;
His presence isn't seasonal,
though some folks act that way.

We don't need to give up Christmas,
or from tradition to depart,
just let the love of Christ, then others,
take first place within our hearts.

2 Corinthians 4:6 "For God, who commanded the light to shine out of darkness, hath shined in our hearts, to give the light of the knowledge of the glory of God in the face of Jesus Christ."

The Things
of
Nature

Spring Morning

Sunlight breaks in the eastern sky, the birds begin to sing,
the morning mist begins to rise as wind chimes in breezes ring.
Another day is dawning, cheerfulness is everywhere,
as all God's little creatures scurry here and there.
Bunnies are discovering new sprouts in the garden patch,
baby birds in nests are calling while others now begin to hatch.
The deer lift up their heads as new scents fill the air,
coyotes making their last calls to neighbors with
whom they share.
Kittens begin to wander out from their hiding place,
while new-born colts kick up their heels as with each other
they do race.

Spring is much abounding, green is everywhere,
newness is upon the earth, things are no longer bare,
for God in wisdom has seen fit to bless us once again
with his miracle of changing seasons that from Genesis did begin.
As wonder springs up all around us, let's praise God for
all he has made,
for he blesses us continually with his promises that do not fade.

*Genesis 1:14 "And God said, 'Let there be lights in the
firmament of the heaven to divide the day from the
night; and let them be for signs, and for seasons and for
days and years.'"*

Spring

As we tire of the winter with it's cold, and snowy days,
there's been mud around us, and the snow has turned to gray.
Then as I look around me, what is this I see?
It seems to have exploded; it's green surrounding me.
Tiny leaves in all their splendor, now adorn the barren trees,
spears of grass in all their glory, sprouting up the sun to see.
Little shoots, where bulbs have been, now break from the ground,
tempting us with thoughts of beauty that later will be found.
Many birds with songs-a-plenty flit from tree to tree,
fill the air with sounds of wonder, as if serenading me.
Smaller creatures come to life, that in a den were hid,
to welcome back spring's warmth, as winter coats they rid.
Children play with much abandon, when freed
from winter's throes,
adults watch, and come to join them, as they their
youthfulness disclose.
Things around are brought to newness, for the winter
they have shed;
thankfulness is all around us as with zeal they look ahead.

Lord, You've created wonder far as the eye can see.
Help us now to praise You; start now Lord, with me.

"For, lo, the winter is past, the rain is over and gone; the flowers appear on the earth; the time of the singing of birds is come, and the voice of the turtle is heard in our land. Song of Solomon 2:11-12

Summer Breeze

Coming gently down the valleys, moving o'er the hills,
rustling leaves in passing, ruffling bunnies for the thrills,
lifting nodding heads of sleepy grass along the way,
picking up leaves here and there, chasing them in play.
Cools the sweat upon our brow, for the sun is warm today,
moves the air around us, we hope it's here to stay.
we see the clouds begin to move slowly across the sky,
we surely are enjoying this slight breeze that's passing by.

This ever elusive current sweeping across the land,
never seen, only heard as it touches things that stand,
causing music to the listening ear as it passes on it's way,
giving us a pause of blessing as it refreshes us today.
Stirring down within our hearts thanksgiving to the Lord,
reminding us that He cares as our temper He's restored.
The wind-chimes of our souls have been stirred today,
thank You Lord for this summer breeze You have sent our way.

Ecclesiastes 1:6 "The wind goeth toward the south, and turneth about unto the north; it whirleth about continually, and the wind returneth again according to his circuits."

Being aware of everything around us, created for our enjoyment, is what makes this life livable. Living in a world of only self would bring us disappointment. Thank God for the breaks He gives to enrich our day.

A Summer Storm

Energy abounds in the heavens, storm clouds are moving in,
gale force winds are sweeping the earth, the rains are soon to begin.
Lightning streaks the horizon, thunder booms through the air,
trees are bowing in reverence as leaves are blown everywhere.
The storm comes in oh so quickly, sheets of rain I now see,
Lord protect those around me, calm spirits of fear within me.

The rain has now changed to a sprinkle, sweet fragrance fills the air,
a rainbow is arched in the sky above, Lord your promise to
us you share.
Calmness moves in all around me, sunbeams shed light everywhere,
birds in the trees are now singing, little streams running here and there.
The grasses are coated with droplets, prisms in the sunlight are made,
colors become so much brighter and children in mud-puddles wade.

Lord we thank you for all of this beauty you've made for our
eyes to behold,
the storm comes before the rainbow just as trials come before the gold.

*The heavens are magnificent. The power of a storm
makes my soul marvel at what God can do. With a sweep
of his hand he can turn chaos into splendor. It reminds
me of what he can do for me if I will let him. "Rejoice in
the Lord always; again I say rejoice."*

Late Fall

Frost upon the window forming patterns of delight.
Snowflakes gently falling, what a mesmerizing sight.
A spider web hangs deserted outside the window pane,
while a bright orange leaf comes drifting, part of summer's last refrain.

They are all things of great beauty, so intricately made,
to fascinate and make memories that will never fade.
They call to our attention the great artist from above
that sculptures these lovely scenes with His mighty hands of love.
He paints the sparkling snowflake each so differently,
we exclaim in joy and wonder if they on our window ledge we see.
He's changed to many colors things that were in summer green,
so we can appreciate His handiwork in this late fall scene.

We thank you Lord for caring, for giving these scenes of joy,
then even on the darkest days, our memories we'll employ.
For what You do is not wasted, I love it very much,
it sets my heart to singing, part of Your loving touch.

He is the lone artist in our daily lives as well,
He's molding us so carefully when in Him we dwell.
He forms us in His likeness starting with our soul,
to ready us for our final home that has become our goal.

*Psalm 37:3 & 4 "Trust in the Lord, and do good; so
shalt thou dwell in the land, and verily thou shalt be fed.
Delight thyself also in the Lord; and he shall give thee
the desires of thine heart."*

Winter Paradise

Trees dressed in icy splendor on a bright and crispy morn,
brown grasses of the fall no longer look forlorn,
for they glisten in the sunlight with a brand-new ice-made coat,
worn with pride for our enjoyment that we can not help but note.
Fence lines guard the frozen land around, shimmering all the while,
eye-sores now are picturesque giving us a chance to smile.
The glazed road with glassy surface daring us to skate
into the wondrous ice-filled world causing us to hesitate
and see the beauty all around that we other times have missed,
giving us a chance to thank the Lord for this scene we can't resist.

Later as the shining sun sends forth it's warming rays
to melt the winter wonderland, it fills our hearts with praise
for this time that was "picture perfect" made to open up our eyes;
Lord you blessed us each and every one with a winter paradise.

Revelation 2:7b "To him who overcometh, I will give to eat of the tree of life, which is in the midst of the paradise of God."

The paradise of God; what a place that must be. God in all his goodness has given us a chance to catch a mere glimpse of what Heaven is like. I feel he gives us marvelous things down here to see and experience just to make us eager for that much more in heaven. Thank You Lord.

Snowflakes

As I'm looking out my window on this cold and snowy day,

I see the great big snowflakes floating as in play.

One lands upon the window screen just for me,

and oh what a wonder in the beauty that I see.

The tiny little crystals brought together one by one

to form the comely snowflake, so unique is every one.

They look as if they're woven with fine silken thread,

to become just a wisp of loveliness, then on the wind are spread

into the air to land on many window sills;

to build a winter blanket on the gardens and the fields,

giving us the moisture that later we will need

for the growing of the grass and the sprouting of the seed

that gives food, or shelter, to sustain our daily lives.

Lord I appreciate the snowflake; it my thankfulness revives.

Isaiah 55:10-11 "For as the rain cometh down, and the snow from heaven, and returneth not thither, but watereth the earth, and maketh it bring forth and bud, that it may give seed to the sower, and bread to the eater: so shall my word be that goeth forth out of my mouth: it shall not return unto me void, but it shall accomplish that which I please, and it shall prosper in the thing whereto I sent it."

Sunrise

Bursting over the East's horizon a big red ball is seen,

casting forth many shadows as the night begins to wane.

Glory breaks through the darkness as sunbeams send out their light,

overcoming all the starlight that has ruled the night.

The moon above is setting, resting for another day,

the sunlight will again God's handiwork display.

Farm roosters start to crowing, the old hen lays her egg,

cows begin their mooing as they for the milking parlor beg.

Highway traffic's moving as cars go place to place,

workers getting ready for their daily jobs to face.

Children rising slowly, sleep still fills their eyes,

looking forward to the day with full energy supplies.

We face the task filled day ahead wondering what will be,

Lord please keep your hand on us is our quiet plea.

Keep us safe, love and care, guide us gently through the day,

we thank you Lord for what you do, with us please have your way.

The sunrise on a cloudless day is magnificent. The world shines in the splendor only God can give. Let's thank Him for the many things we take for granted that He has given us in nature.

Evening

Evening casts its shadows at the closing of the day,

the sun sends forth its descending rays in a wonderful display,

for it hides behind a clouded bank spraying color everywhere,

painting a sky filled canvas that will to nothing else compare.

God gives us this special view to ease away the day,

to give us rest from all the toils that have come our way.

When we take time to notice then He our weariness dispels,

for we breathe a prayer of thankfulness for these beautiful pastels.

The breeze that rustles in the trees join us to praise His name,

while crickets, frogs and locust give voice to do the same.

The hooting of a big owl, the cooing of the dove,

make the scene more joyful as they send to Him their love.

God has been so good to us more than we can comprehend,

for He has given us abiding love and is our unfailing friend.

Though our day may have been hectic, God will reach out His hand and wipe away all our cares. He will relieve us of any burden that we are carrying if we will let Him. As we look in His face as the evening casts its shadows we will realize that there is no other like Him.

Lord, thank You for Your faithfulness to us.

Sunset

Clouds gather on the west's horizon, reflecting the evening sun,

causing lights of many colors, gold with purple, pink and cinnamon.

Another day had ended, with God's grace we've carried on

through the many daily happenings since we wakened with the dawn.

Evening shadows 'round us gather giving up the day,

like a blanket to enfold us affording rest from work and play.

The moon above begins it's journey across the starlit sky,

assuring us of safety under God's ever watchful eye.

The creatures of the night begin scurrying here and there,

they too, are surrounded with God's never ending care.

God we ask for your protection as we cross into the night.

May our rest in you be certain and our dreams be a delight.

Let your tenderness encompass 'round about us as we lay,

hold us close and give us comfort until the break of day.

Proverbs 3:24-26 "When thou liest down, thou shalt not be afraid: yea, thou shalt lie down, and thy sleep shall be sweet. Be not afraid of sudden fear, neither of the desolation of the wicked, when it cometh. For the Lord shall be thy confidence, and shall keep thy foot from being taken."

Moonlight

As I look across the land on a bright and moonlight night,
everything in sight is wondrously displayed.
So clean and clear and lovely, bathed in a gentle glow,
as if the landscape were of gold, or silver made.
The things I take for granted, or that in daylight are a pain,
become mellow when they've slipped into the night.
As they're viewed within the circle of the moonlight's
golden beams,
then become to me a thing of great delight.
The heavens up above are a beauty to behold,
as the stars in all their glory are arrayed,
a cluster over here, or one shooting over there,
chasing down a moonbeam that has strayed.

I find within myself a joy that cannot be contained,
with a reverence far deeper than my words can tell.
I know that God above has blessed me on this night,
to let me know that when I'm with him, all is well.
I want to thank you Lord for showing me you care,
by giving me this welcome picture to enjoy.
By pouring out your love you build a faith in me,
that nothing interfering will destroy.

*Ephesians 3:17b-19 "And I pray that you being rooted,
and established in love, may have power, together with all
the saints, to grasp how wide, and long, and high, and
deep is the love of Christ, and to know this love that
surpasses knowledge--that you may be filled to the
measure of all the fullness of God."*

48

The Stars

Like a big umbrella that guards the night sky
are the stars out in numbers above.
They protect by their light from shadows of fear
as they wrap me in peace and in love.
They twinkle in majestic splendor that glows
from dusk to the dawning of day,
giving assurance at morn that all has gone well
through the night as they've lighted the way.

My heart overflows with thanksgiving and praise
to the Lord as I enter the night,
for I know without doubting that His love for me
won't diminish as the rays of sunlight.
For He has given to me this wonderful sky
bright with His promises true
that He'll care for me from time until time
as I trust Him in all I pursue.

The skies are a wonder to behold. I feel sorry for the ones that have missed the opportunity to view the skies of the wide open spaces. God has indeed given us a canopy of love. Though we all may not be given the same view, God himself is the same to all of us.

Daniel 12:3 "And they that be wise shall shine as the brightness of the firmament; and they that turn many to righteousness as the stars for ever and ever."

The Rose

The rose, a much desired flower, opens gently from the start
showing just a bit of color that goes clear to the heart.

As it's beauty begins to emerge it fascinates watchful eyes,
the fragrance coming from within we much desire and prize,
for it fills the air 'round about with a scent that comes
from heaven,
giving those passing by a lift to the spirit in them.

When it opens in maturity, velvet petals to be seen,
joy for life is given viewers as they from it's beauty glean.

Thorns are the protection God has given all,
to shield self from dangers that to each life befall.
They are warning to those in passing that they the
loveliness would spoil,
if care in handling is not given to this precious flower royal.

Life is like the rose we're given to enjoy for just a season,
for it passes by in God's own time, but it's given us with reason.
We're to live it to the fullest as God shows us the way,
that we'll understand more fully if we worship, praise and pray.
He will keep our life in beauty with hope for a future bright,
for He's promised us His caring when in Him we do delight.

The rose is a flower of distinction. It is given when there is sorrow, when forgiveness is needed, in celebration and in love. When I see a rose my heart melts.
We are roses in God's garden of life. Our love to Him is a pleasing fragrance. Our praises to Him are our beauty. We are a variety of colors and sizes to enhance the garden. May we always please Him.

Dandelions,
Pretty Little Flowers

You pretty little flowers popped up everywhere I see,
dot the country side for miles around, so wild and so free.
Your face so like the sun itself, turned up to the sky,
praising God through out your days, until you have to die.
You're much maligned and talked about, some think
you're just a weed,
but carried to Mom in a child's hand, fulfills a loving need.
You become the gold that you portray, a gift from paradise,
a heart is filled with cherished thoughts not sold for any price.

You're sprayed and cut and dug up, you're hardy and you try,
the temptation to just give up seems to pass you by.
If we followed your example, think how strong that we would be,
God would be so proud of us, don't you agree?

Little dandelion, pretty little flower, don't let folks put you down,
your name has spread through out the land, you've
become renown.
God made you just as you're to be, we can't take that away
and from the looks of the yards around, you are here to stay.
If folks knew that I cared for you, they would think I'm not bright,
but if they could see you like I do, they'd know that
God was right.

*God has blessed us each one with the inherent
ability to see things differently. Each eye captures nature
in a unique way. Thank You Lord for this gift.*

Seeing Beauty

As I woke early this morning, the daylight greeted me.
As I looked out through the window, there were wondrous things to see,
the trees in all their splendor, leafed arms raised up to the sky,
the flower's bright heads were nodding in a slight breeze passing by,
tiny lights above were fading, remnants of a starry night,
while the grass with many dewdrops, danced and shimmered
in the light.

There are many things of beauty God has made for us to see,
with our open hearts he'll lead us to whatever it will be.
It may be to our neighbor or someone down the block,
or it could be that one person we've avoided while on walks.
Beauty is for the beholder, if we through God's eyes will see.
Let us not by choice be blinded; show your beauty Lord to me.

Romans 15:7 *"Wherefore receive ye one another, as Christ also received us to the glory of God."*

My
Favorites

To most of us, the home of our childhood is very important. My childhood was spent in the Sandhills of Nebraska. Some folks call them "God forsaken." To me they are "God's country." It is all in where God has placed the heart.

I am looking to the future with a home in heaven. Although I have been given a small taste of heaven here, nothing will compare to the home that God has prepared for them that truly know and love Him.

The Nebraska Sandhills

As the cows graze sweet grass on the hillside
and the breeze turns the windmill below,
I'm amazed at the quiet and beauty,
it's a sight I will never outgrow.
The sandhills completely surround me,
the sky oh, so blue overhead,
the calves in the valley are playing
with the shadows a few clouds shed.
I have a feeling of peace and comfort
as I view the wonders that God has made,
I'm aware of His wonderful presence
in the things I for nothing would trade.

The Bible talks to us about heaven
with it's streets all paved in pure gold,
and the foundations of precious gemstones
are a beauty to behold.
The gates are pearls of a great size,
so large I cannot comprehend,
no sun, moon, or stars are needed
for God is the light therein.

There comes to my mind a question,
what other things up there will I see?
Will there be sandhills in heaven?
For they're heaven on earth to me.

There are so many stresses in our lives today that God has given us each a pastime where we can come to grips with reality. We need to lean back and rest against Him, letting all our cares and worries ease out of our lives. He will put His loving arms around us, holding us against the storms that we have been facing and setting us on the rock of steadiness and letting our feet rest in the sand of relaxation. We can wiggle our toes digging deeper into real living while holding our fishing pole baited with desire for a closer walk with Him. Then He will give us a peaceful sleep with pleasant dreams of His goodness, building our strength for the days ahead.

God is so good!

Gone Fishin'

O, I look unto the day when it can be said
that I have gone a fishin' and took my camper for a bed.
I see myself relaxin' in a chair down by the lake
with just some worms and a fishin' pole, what a lucky break.
The lake is so relaxin', wild sounds around are heard,
frogs and crickets, bees a buzzin' and the singin' of the birds.
When the water is a lappin' against the sandy bank
my cares just go a scootin' and I have God to thank.
The trees around are rustlin' with the breezes passin' by
and the ground squirrel beside me playin' is so easy on the eye.
The sunrise O, so pleasin', the sunset heaven sent,
makes me want to stick around and put a sign out
"House for rent."
I know that God made these places for folks like me that be,
'cause we then seem even closer to each other, Him and me.
He gave the sights, and sounds, and smells,
to put the mind at ease,
and a fish to catch now and again the fisherman to please.
I thank You God for this dream now please make it reality,
'cause I'd like to go a fishin', just my camper, You and me.

Music boxes come in every shape and size. I have wooden ones with lids. My mother-in-law has a beautiful carousel horse. They each play such joyful music. They are little pick-me-ups in times of stress or when the memory of a loved one that has given it to you comes to mind. Special occasions are generally tied in with the gift. So much enjoyment can be had from such a pretty little object.

God gives us the simple things in life. He created the music we like so much. The right kind can bring us closer to him. He likes to see us happy.

The Music Box

'Round and 'round the dancer goes never it's place to leave,
standing forever all alone in a land of make believe.
Depending on the tender touch winding from below
the spring to tighten then release to start the music flow.
Going always and unendingly to the same enchanting tune,
ever turning, gracefully poised, with our heartstrings to commune.
It may be standing on a shelf or wrapped and hid away,
but it's ready at our slightest whim to let it's music play.
For we are the master and it the slave in the partnership that's formed,
but we are one in a common bond when the dancing is performed.
We let our hearts and minds become caught in the world of dreams,
as we watch the dancer whirl and spin to our favorite music themes.
Then as it's winding slowly down we place it once again,
away with pleasant memories of what were or might have been.
We return again to our own world ready to face the day,
thankful for the slight reprieve that has come our way.

Little dancer, dance again when in our heart we feel the need,
for we are true companions when we from our cares are freed.

I'm sure God has a sense of humor. There are many things in life that can make us laugh, especially when we look back on them. The little mouse was a highlighted experience in my life and I have enjoyed the thoughts of him for many years. It is an experience that I will probably never have again.

I hear God laughing yet.

The Mouse

The children were all tucked in bed, Mom on the couch was sitting,
the little dog lay on the floor either asleep or meditating.
They were gazing at the T.V. resting quietly from the day
when the little creature joined them like it had always been that way.
His look was quizzical and beguiling as he sat there on the floor,
taking in the things around like he'd done it much before.
He wasn't the least little bit afraid of Mom or of the dog,
he sat there just as quiet as if he were a bump upon a log.
He watched the entertainment, he watched them get a snack,
he watched them walk around the house, he stayed till they came back.
Mom kept her eye upon the little guy although she thought it queer,
he seemed to fit in with the rest as if he were their peer.
In any other circumstance Mom would have set a trap,
but this one was to good to be true, he was a spunky little chap.
She turned out the light, went upstairs to bed without another thought,
decided that on another day was soon enough for him to be caught.
Next evening came, they did the same and much to their surprise
the little visitor joined them again with a twinkle in his eyes.
This odd occurrence went for many nights, the guest always
took his place
beside the couch to enjoy himself in his own little tiny space.

God called to my attention what an odd trio we must be,
myself, the dog and a little gray mouse, I know He smiled at me.

A heritage left to me by my Grandmother was her words; "Be proud of your age!" and that has never left me. I feel I have earned every grey hair and wrinkle. My life is nothing to be ashamed of so neither should be my age. It is given to me by God.

Proverbs 16:31 "The hoary (grey) head is a crown of glory, if it be found in the way of righteousness. 20:29 The glory of young men is their strength: and the beauty of the old men is the grey head."
Isaiah 40:31 "But they that wait upon the Lord shall renew their strength; they shall mount up with wings as eagles; they shall run and not be weary; and they shall walk and not faint."

Experiencing Life

White has overcome my hair's dark tones,
wrinkles appearing everywhere,
muscles not what they used to be,
where, oh where did I error.
My spirit is the same as yesterday,
for I was a teenager then,
my thoughts are no older in essence,
though wiser, I'm sure, "amen".
Experience has been a good teacher,
but I was sure I knew all those days,
now grandchildren are entering that circle,
I laugh at the error of their ways.
My mirror, though a friend, is too truthful,
I sometimes don't like what I see,
I work to change the appearance,
but I am still just me.
Then I realize God had blessed me,
I'm now much closer to home;
my spirit begins soaring,
for he will not leave me alone.
I fly now with wings of an eagle,
God has shown me the way,
my teens are now but a memory,
and life is ahead this day.
The future is brighter and brighter,
I fear not what is ahead,
I know that whatever besets me
I will face without dread.
For God is going before me,
he's smoothing my road day by day,
my path has been made certain,
Thank you Lord for leading the way.
Aging is no longer a factor,
I'm proud of where I have been.
Come on life, let's get going;
just show me where and when.

Dear Lord

When night is past, the day I see,
things of yesterday a trouble be,
clear my mind, make it free,
show yourself, Dear Lord, to me.

Clouds roll in, your face obscure,
talk around makes me unsure,
trials come, help is my plea,
show yourself, Dear Lord, to me.

Friends turn away, I don't know why,
feel all I can do is cry,
depression comes, I have to flee,
show yourself, Dear Lord, to me.

I smile to cover things inside,
yet thoughts torment, I cannot hide,
I struggle to come close to thee,
show yourself, Dear Lord, to me.

When I've reached deepest despair,
I notice you've been standing there,
with peace, and comfort awaiting me,
you've shown yourself, Dear Lord, to me.

God
In Our
Everyday
Lives

The Bible

It's the most read book in the book store, it's on the best seller list,
with use it becomes frayed and crumbles, it is one that would be missed.
Some leave it on the table to read as they sit in bed,
to others it's a dust collector, it is hardly ever read.
To the Christian it's a lifeline, with prayer we come to know the Lord,
we learn of His desires and commandments as we function
in one accord.
It is our owners manual, it will keep our life well tuned,
it will give us joy and comfort when we with the Lord have communed.
It is God's final authority, it will tell us what's right and wrong,
when we follow it to the letter, it will make us strong.
We can't use just part to get by, we must use the whole book,
for taken out of context, there is much we would overlook.
Then it would let our life get sidetracked, for we won't know
what is real,
we would miss what God has for us, Satan could our life steal.

Pray that God would give you insight to what He has for you,
you'll be assured He means just what He says and His answers
will come through.
Take the Bible seriously, it'll light your path each day,
if you'll read as God intended, from Him you will never stray.

*Psalm 119:10 "Thy word is a lamp unto my feet,
and a light unto my path."*

Prayer

Prayer is conversation, a time of talking with the Lord.

It's heart communication that has it's own reward.

Some feel it's a necessity just when things are going bad,

or that it's only what they need to do when they're feeling sad.

We're to pray continually, that's what the Bible says to do,

to be in constant contact with a friend who's always true.

Take the time to chat awhile about the smaller things;

take the time to praise Him, you'll be surprised at the peace it brings.

Thank Him for the answers that you are going to see,

even though there will be times that you don't agree.

God knows what He's doing, and it's always for our best,

although we may not see it, and it puts our trusting to a test.

He is our Heavenly Father, our brother, our best friend,

and talking to Him always, brings a closeness, a heartfelt blend.

He will be your lifeline everyday your whole life through;

take the time, give Him a chance, He will your heart renew.

1 Thessalonians 5:17 "Pray without ceasing."

Luke 18:1 "And he spake a parable unto them to this end, that men ought always to pray, and not to faint."

Morning Prayer

It's such a gray day, my spirits are low, I'd like to stay in bed,
I'd be in much more comfort with the covers thrown over my head.
A still small voice comes to me, my feet then hit the floor,
for God has spoken to me, for me He has much more.

I take my Bible from the bedside, I read a chapter or two,
I begin to get excited over what my God can do.
I bow my head in prayer and ask His guidance with my day,
for His hand to be upon me, that in my life He'll have His own way.

Breakfast becomes a disaster, the kids will be late for school,
we fought about their clothing, what I wanted wasn't "cool."
Then for a fleeting moment God laid His hand upon me,
I wasn't doing things His way, "forgive me" is my plea.

I got a call from the neighbor, "Have lunch with me today."
Going out in this cold and wet, caused me my answer to delay.
Then I felt God prodding, "She needs you very much."
My answer was a joyous one, for I had felt God's touch.

She told me she was troubled, we bowed our head in prayer,
God's love did surround us, we knew that He was there.
I knew I'd done the right thing, God made me aware
that all He'd done was give answer to my morning prayer.

When you ask God's guidance, remember He'll be true,
He'll give you the answer that's tailored just for you.
Always do His bidding, He'll show you the way,
may He now go with you, have a glorious love filled day.

Do You Believe?

If someone asked "Do you believe in prayer?"
what answer would you give?
Would you say "Yes" to get them off your back,
or is it yes by the way you live?
Is the answer given, come from in the head,
or is it real unto your heart?
If a need arose, would you know what to do,
or would you faint and fall apart?

Do you know that prayer is how we talk to God;
just say what's on your mind.
You can talk to him like you would to me,
or to your neighbor out behind.
He is always near, you don't have to find
someone to hear you out,
you just talk to him right on the spot
about your problems, or your doubt.
Tell him about your varied attitudes,
or things that bother you;
talk to him about the day ahead,
or something you need to do.
Speak to him of lovely flowers you see,
or the pretty day today;
let him know how you appreciate
the differences along your way.
Thank him for the things he's done,
your burdens to relieve;
let him know, and those 'round about,
that in prayer you do believe.

Philippians 2:13-15 "For it is God which worketh in you both to will and to do of his good pleasure. Do all things without murmurings and disputings: that ye may be blameless and harmless, the sons of God, without rebuke, in the midst of a crooked and perverse nation, among whom ye shine as lights in the world."
Ephesians 4:1-2 "Therefore, the prisoner of the Lord, beseech you that ye walk worthy of the vocation wherewith ye are called, with all lowliness and meekness, with longsuffering, forbearing one another in love."

God's Call

It may be in a quiet voice, or a feeling deep inside,
it may be more dramatic, something from which we cannot hide,
it could be from the reading of his ever holy word,
leading us to listen to things that before we've heard.
Whatever way it comes to us, please don't put on hold, or stall,
for we by God are chosen, we have heard God's call.

It may be to a mission field, or to a church we have to go,
it could be that he wants our voice to sing of what we know.
He may need us to teach the children in our Sunday School,
or reach others that we meet, by living the golden rule.
He may give us a talent that's not had by all,
do what he asks us to do, we have heard God's call.

Just as vital are the tasks we are to do from day to day,
the ones we know as little things that have come our way.
We may go to see our neighbor to lend a helping hand,
or give when something's happened that we have not planned.
These we do not thinking and sometimes we don't recall,
but even in the small things, we have heard God's call.

The things we may not think about as a calling from the Lord,
are the things we've chosen now to do, goals we move toward,
the life we've been given now to live, or talents we've pursued,
the work in our chosen field, or our job we too, include.
When we've been given talent, or desire and ask God's
blessing on them all,
then we can be assured by him, that we have listened
to God's call.

The Bottom Line

We have been given the "Ten Commandments" to live by day to day.
We have been given "The Lord's Prayer" to teach us how to pray.
We have been given the "Beatitudes" to show right choices will be blessed.
The "Proverbs" are to guide us with help of wisdom to address.
The "Psalm" teach praise and worship, as we cry out to the Lord,
There are also many places that give insight to our reward.

People have a tendency to interpret these things their own way,
"God and Bible get in line with me, then I can go and play."
They don't like the way God spelled it out, their conscience gets upset,
But remember that He has the "last word," your life you could regret.
If you love your God with all your heart, with all your soul, and mind,
Love your neighbor as yourself, then all else will fall in line.

Believe that Christ was God's only Son, that he gave his life for you,
Repent of sin, accept God's love, your life he will renew.
Read God's word, the Bible, let it be to you "sunshine,"
Then eternal life in heaven will be the "Bottom Line."

Matthew 22:37-40 "Jesus said unto him, 'Thou shalt love the Lord thy God with all thy heart, and with all thy soul, and with all thy mind. This is the first and greatest commandment. And the second is like unto it, Thou shalt love thy neighbor as thyself. On these two commandments hang all the law and the prophets.'"

Sweet Peace

I have a nagging worry, it's just a little thing,
it's bogged down in my mind, it does upset to me bring.
I discuss it with a friend, but the words just won't console,
I hang on with all my might, seems real worry is my goal.
I go on about my day, trouble rears it's head,
a person down the block got hurt with what another said.
I was called in for a conference, I think gossip was the cause,
it now sticks down within my mind, against such things
there must be laws.
The kids have gone away to school, we only talk by phone,
I'm in the house all by myself, I'm feeling quite alone.
My best friend was walking down the street, passed right by my door,
never even looked my way, that's never been before.
Made me upset with the world, I wondered what was wrong,
knew she must be mad at me, the feeling was so strong.

The devil's had a heyday, all his fun at my expense,
I needed something to help me, someone for my defense.
Peace has been taken from me, I cannot see God's face,
I need to hide within His love, I need to know His grace.
I falter as I try to pray, God seems so far away,
in desperation I call out for His help for the rest of the day.
Then it comes so gently, I begin to feel the flow,
peace is washing over me from my head down to my toe.
I relax as I feel the comfort of His unconditional love,
sweet peace has come into my being as it's poured from God above.
Peace, sweet peace, He's given me, I now freely praise His name,
for now all the world is fine with me, the devil lost this game.

Psalm 85:10 "Mercy and truth are met together; right-eousness and peace have kissed each other."

Psalm 34:1-3
"I will bless the Lord at all times:
his praise shall continually be in my mouth.
My soul shall make her boast in the Lord:
the humble shall hear thereof, and be glad.
O magnify the Lord with me,
and let us exalt his name together."

As We Praise Him

Rivers of praise flow through my soul as I'm worshiping the Lord.
I tell Him how much He means to me, that He is my adored.
I lift my hands in thanksgiving for what He has done for me,
He fills my very being, He sets my bound spirit free.
He's delivered me from the chaos that does in this world abound,
I've found the secret of life that can only in Him be found.
He makes me happy beyond measure, He makes me know I'm alive,
He lets me enjoy all life's pleasures as He does my spirit revive.
He brings to my mind the small things He's created for me to see,
He holds in His hand the tempest that would try to overcome me.
He sits me on His footstool to tell me He loves me so,
then He reaches out to touch me before I have to go
about the daily business He has given me to do,
He gives me a different outlook, He gives me a whole new view.

Come, let's join together in the reading of His word,
He will show us many new things in what we've already heard.
He won't leave us distracted, He'll bring together things we should know,
He'll touch us where we are hurting, because He loves us so.
When we take time in His presence, He will bless our soul,
then He'll spend the day beside us, help us achieve our goal.

Thank You Lord for the abundance You have sent our way,
with our praises we now bless You, thank you for this day.

Lamentations 3:22-23 "It is of the Lord's mercies that we are not consumed, because his compassions fail not. They are new every morning: great is thy faithfulness."
Proverbs 21:21 "He that followeth after righteousness and mercy findeth life, righteousness, and honor."

A New Beginning

Wake up you sleepy head, open your eyes,
a new day has begun.
Robed in the splendor of a cloudless sky
are the rays of the morning sun.
It has come to bathe the earth for you
in the life-giving light of day.
Breathe the air, fill your lungs,
there's no longer time to delay.
Set priorities right, think ahead,
what goal for life will you set?
What will you do with the time you're given,
to what will you say "not yet"?
You have choices to make, it is up to you,
have you turned to the Lord?
Are you starting your day by talking to him,
or by reading from the Word?
This day is important, more than you may know,
so how do you begin?
Get it right from the start, take a little time,
before other things close in.
A helping hand should be welcome,
a clear mind should be a desire,
strength for the day an urgent request
as many hard things do transpire.
A shield from wrong thoughts and actions
as worldly things cross your path,
would be a blessing worth asking for
and save you from other's wrath.
Guidance from one thing to another,
a smoother transition would be
something that help from your loving Lord
would be worth the plea.
Remember to thank Him for helping
as you don't want to go it alone,
you'll feel better, I'll grant you,
when you make your appreciation known.
Now that you've started out on the right foot,
ready to face good or strife,
you've been given a new beginning,
this is the first day of the rest of your life.

Golden Nuggets From God

Golden nuggets to people have been an interest since time began.
Inherent greed within them that is not confined to just man.
All the animal kingdom want for themselves the very best
of what nature has to offer, it is a continual quest.
They spy, they chase, they catch, they fight amongst themselves,
grass is greener across the fence, we're just as bad ourselves.
Searching, always searching, always wanting for ourselves more,
most never realizing what God has for them in store.
God gave to us the little things to enrich our lives each day,
things we don't give much thought to, as we go along our way.
A smile from someone we love, or a handshake
or the hug of a friend,
the wag of a puppy-dogs tail in greeting, are nuggets
that God does send.
He gives us the sunrise and sunset, the dewdrops
that shimmer and glow,
He gives us birds to sing to us, little arms that loves us so.
He gives us the hoot of the owl, He gives us the stars at night,
He gives us the scent of flowers and the rainbow
so pretty and bright.
He gives us the voice of a child saying it's nightly prayers,
He gives us time to enjoy ourselves, He gives a heart to care.
He gives us a song in our heart, He gives us feelings
for each other,
He gives us childhood sweethearts, He gives us a
Father and Mother.
God has been so good to us, even His Son to us He gave,
so we can have a home in heaven, when we let Him our soul save.
To us He charges no interest, all to us is eternally free,
let's be thankful for God's golden nuggets, He loves us,
don't you agree?

Walking With The Lord

Things are going so good this morning,
the sun is shining so bright,
I've done my Bible study and prayer,
this day will be my delight.
The birds song seems cheerier than usual,
they match the song in my heart,
I felt in my mind a prick from Satan,
but God's word deflected his dart.
This day seems better than my other days,
peace in my life has been poured,
I started the day the way I always should,
now I'm walking with the Lord.

This afternoon has proved to be different,
trouble has showed its head,
I got the mail and a telephone call
that have made my heart feel dread.
It's something I've been expecting,
no problems did I foresee,
there was a mistake made somewhere,
now it is gnawing at me.
I went to prayer with a heavy burden,
peace to me is now restored,
God again to me has been faithful,
for I'm walking with the Lord.

Read your Bible and pray in the morning
at the beginning of your day.
It'll get things started on the right foot
and will help them stay that way.
You'll find more peace than you've dreamed of,
the Devil will miss his fun,
for you've girded yourself with God's armor,
putting Satan on the run.
He's a coward come to you in wolf's clothing,
he'll come beating on your door,
the Word stands between you and him
and you have now declared war.
He'll run away from you whining and crying,
a hit by God has been scored,
peace for you is still reigning,
for you are walking with the Lord.

Our Dream

This nation where we live today, was founded on a dream;
dream of freedom, of respect, where God could reign supreme.
They fought to keep the dream alive, expanding all the while,
pushing back the great frontier mile after dusty mile.
Though rough and tumble was the life, surviving day to day,
the love of God, too, forged ahead, helping smooth the way.
Some things were faced that only God could help to bring them through,
things we wonder what we'd have done had it been me, or you.

We face again from time to time, things that try this dream to shatter,
man made ideas, or selfish acts, telling us God doesn't matter.
They go against God's holy word, telling us it's "status quo,"
that we can have things our own way, because we want it so.

Real dreams of family centered life, where God can be the head,
where he guides us in the things we do and in the things that's said
are scorned and pushed aside by those who haven't got a clue
to what God is really all about, what he can really do.

Let's forge ahead, lead the way, lift our nation up in prayer,
ask God to help us out again, our beginning dream repair.
Ask him what we need to do to set our nation right,
then press ahead step at a time, the dream held in our sight.
Don't give up, do what we can starting with today,
give ourselves back to God, then he will lead the way.

*Psalm 5:11-12   "But let all those that put their trust in
thee rejoice: let them ever shout for joy, because thou
defendest them: let them also that love thy name be joyful
in thee.   For thou, Lord, wilt bless the righteous; with
favor wilt thou compass him as with a shield."*

Tears!

There are tears of sorrow, tears of joy,
tears when hurting, or tears of ploy,
Tears some feel it is but a curse,
others love them, it could be worse.
Tears when your newborn baby cried,
tears when your daughter became a bride,
tears when a little one said it's first word,
tears when at his program he could be heard.
tears at the first time going to school,
tears when you've made of yourself a fool.
Tears of compassion fill the eyes,
when a friend has come for your advice,
or just there for your listening ear,
you cry together, you share a tear.
Tears are glue to mend a broken heart,
when you feel your world's been torn apart.

Tears will always have their place,
and when you see them streaming down the face
of one who's sought to change their goal,
by shedding tears that wash and cleanse the soul,
we praise the Lord for His saving grace
when we see His joy and presence fill a face.

Tears, more tears may we feel free,
for they can show we care for the things that be.

*Psalm 126:5-6 "They that sow in tears shall reap in joy.
He that goeth forth and weepeth, bearing precious seed,
shall doubtless come again with rejoicing, bringing his
sheaves with him.."*

Time

Time, an invaluable commodity, is given us each day.
God allots to us this given amount so we can mark it off and say
this much I give to this or that to keep record of what we do
with our life as we move along, then tomorrow we start anew.
We mark it by a time clock, or a clock upon a shelf,
it may be one upon our wrist, or like a grandfather standing by itself.

Moment by moment it passes on, second at a time,
what are you doing with yours, what have I done with mine?
Time is so elusive, it's here for a second and then gone,
forever into eternity, and then we must move on.
It never will be returned to us, it has sped along its way,
we have to make the most of it as we forfeit with delay.

Time belongs to God alone, just so much to each He lends,
we have to make the most of it, for our life on it depends.
We don't know what we've been given, in a moment it may slip away,
Have we done what God would have us do, have we
honored Him today?
If we make mistakes along the way we can ask Him to forgive,
then make the most of our time that's left, as life in Him we live.
If we ask Him to lead and guide each day, to keep us in His way,
when our time is used and we leave this life we'll forever with Him stay.

Romans 13:11 "And that, knowing the time, that now is the high time to awake out of sleep: for now is our salvation nearer than when we believed."

Time waits for no man. It moves on in God's control. We can only have what we use. The other is lost to us for eternity. May we use it for God's glory. That time will leave no regrets.

Wasted Time

What's happened to the time today; we have been so busy
that we haven't taken time to rest; the speed has made us dizzy.
We oft times feel guilty if we haven't kept the pace
of everything around us that we see in life's "rat race."
Any less would show we're "lazy" and would be a crime,
but how much of what we've done is really wasted time?

We took the time to sit awhile, visited with someone we know,
about little things around us, oh how the words did flow.
We discussed world situations, the neighbors down the way,
our children with their problems, or what our friends might say.
We did no harm to others, we felt our visit was well-timed,
but how much was unto the Lord; how much was wasted time?

We are held accountable for all things we do or say;
let's take some time to ask the Lord to help us with our day.
He can be there with us in everything we need to do,
to guide our conversation, to give us a worthwhile view.
Let's relax within his caring, his help to us is prime,
let's be aware, when it's unto the Lord, it's never wasted time.

Psalm 90:12 "So teach us to number our days, that we may apply our hearts unto wisdom."
Ephesians 5:15-17 "See then that ye walk circumspectly, not as fools, but as wise, redeeming the time, because the days are evil. Wherefore be ye not unwise, but understanding what the will of the Lord is.

Love Others
As I Have Loved You!

He stood alone on the corner, a rag-tag sort of guy,
his clothes showed many wearings, you passed, he just said "Hi!"
You ducked your head no knowing what you were to do,
then the Word of God came to you, "Love others as I have loved you!"

She stumbled as you saw her swaying here and there,
she'd been sipping on a bottle, she held it tight in fear.
You rushed to get on by her, she smelled so of the brew,
then the Lord spoke to your heart, "Love others as I have loved you!"

They were two little ornery children, you could see there was no love,
their actions were atrocious, you knew yours were a cut-above,
you took your children elsewhere, you hoped those would
get their just due,
then God stopped you in your very tracks, "Love others as
I have loved you!"

They came to your church that Sunday, their clothes were
old and soiled,
their car was a virtual "rust bucket," they smelled of food
that was spoiled.
they moved together down the aisle deciding to sit in your pew,
the Spirit placed His hand upon you, "Love others as I have loved you!"

Your conscience has been a bother, with others you do not share,
the Lord has been speaking to you, of many things you're
becoming aware.
You've decided to yield to Gods spirit, He's given you a whole new view,
with His love He does enfold you and says: "Love others as
I have loved you!"

*John 13:34 "A new commandment I give unto you, that ye love one
another; as I have loved you, that ye also love one another."*
      *As Christ's love flows into us, it will flow from us to others. Even
those we consider to be unlovable will become lovable to us. It will be the
love of Christ. Oh, to be like Jesus.*

84

Making The Choice

A choice is something we make for everything that we do.
Some folks don't understand, it's important and it's true.
We make the choice to use our tongue, what we say belongs to us,
to use our temper whether or no, or whether we cause a fuss.
If we decide to smile or not, or what attitude we will use,
is the choice that we have made, it is up to us which way we pursue.
It's as simple as one, two, three, if we understand,
we don't have to do the things that the big "I" demands.
We can choose to do things God's way, or we can wing it on our own,
we are held responsible, for the choice is ours alone.
We may follow in others footsteps, but it is the way we choose,
we can choose to think on our own or emulate others views.
God gave us each a mind, He gave us a will of our own,
He made us individual, He gave us our own backbone.
We can be wishy-washy, or we can choose to be strong,
we can choose the right way to go, or we can choose for wrong.
If we study God's word, the Bible, He will show us the way we should go,
but the ultimate choice is up to us, we can't say we didn't know.
Take some time to think for awhile, decide upon your goal,
then follow the course that you choose, it is under your control.

God will give us help if we ask Him, He won't make us go it alone.
He gave us prayer to communicate with Him, it's closer than our telephone.
Just speak right out, tell Him your need, then listen for His reply,
you won't be sorry when you lean on Him, for on Him you can always rely.

Proverbs 8:10-11
"Receive my instruction, and not silver;
and knowledge rather than choice gold.
For wisdom is better than rubies;
and all the things that may be desired
are not compared to it."

Responsibility

"Pretty is as pretty does,"
is a phrase my Grandma used.
It was meant to teach a child she loved
which was the proper way to choose.
We need to know we're responsible
for the choices that we make,
that we are also responsible
for the action that we take.
We can't blame others for the things we do,
for the actions are really ours,
the things we say are the words we choose,
as the tongue is in our power.
We can't really pass the buck,
or behind others can we hide,
for our actions tell the real truth
of what is down inside.
If we choose to practice the things we see,
or the things we read or hear,
that is what we will become,
as to those things we adhere.
Let us take a look within ourselves
to see what is really there,
for we are our responsibility
in the things we do and share.

Proverbs 16:16 "How much better is it to get wisdom than gold! and to get understanding rather to be chosen than silver!"

It Really Could Be You

Have you lately caught yourself saying "tell me, have you heard,"
to what to you is a little thing, so that others hear your every word?
Did you give it just a little twist to make it sound more true?
What if the shoe were on the other foot; what if it were you?

If there's a story going 'round that's so pleasing to the ear,
is there really truth to it, or just what you like to hear?
Take your time, think a bit before you let it through.
What if the shoe were on the other foot; what if it were you?

The story really could be true; shouldn't you call a spade, a spade?
Think again, ask yourself is it truth, or from fiction made?
Do you really want to be the one to ruin a life, or two?
What if the shoe were on the other foot; what if it were you?

There are some things that are true, but for you there is no part;
Do you want to spread it 'round, or keep it in your heart?
What if it were about your best friend, then what would you do?
What if the shoe were on the other foot; what if it were you?

There are times that in this life, you hear things the way they are,
but even then, sometimes they're heard with a twist that reputations mar.
Would God be pleased with you today, if you told a story to
only one, or two?
What if the shoe were on the other foot; what if it were you?

Stories can get so out of hand as they're passed from ear to ear.
If they're about the ones you love, is it what you want to hear?
Pray, instead, for the one who's hurt, ask God to help them through.
Remember; the shoe could be on your foot; it really could be you.

Touching Lives
For Eternity's Sake

Before Christ left He gave a command,
"Go out, tell the whole earth,"
about His love, the blood He shed
and the offer of new spiritual birth
to all who will come to repent of sin,
taking Him for their Lord
over everything in this way of life
and making Him their adored.
We can go to our next door neighbor,
or ones who are in jail,
we may go to another town,
or send a letter in the mail.
We might go as a missionary,
or give to send sisters or brothers
to a distant land to spread the good news
that Christ died for all others.

We need awareness of what is around us,
as we seek to do His will,
to feel for those that are hurting,
to reach to those He would fill.
We hold in our hand a lifeline
for those who are drowning in sin,
we need the courage to save them,
as their lives for Him we win.
We must tune our hearts to His wave length,
the souls of the world are at stake,
we must be ready and willing,
for we're touching lives for eternity's sake.

Mark 16:15-16 "And he said unto them, 'Go ye into all the world, and preach the gospel to every creature. He that believeth and is baptized shall be saved; but he that believeth not shall be damned.'"

Comfort Zone

Comfort zone is the place to be,
it's where we sit so comfortably.
We're well rutted, we don't fall,
    things don't bother us at all.

Neighbors hurting, children cry,
homeless out there wonder why
we don't help them, do we care?
In our comfort we're unaware.

Lord shake us up, set us free,
this is not like we want to be.
Helping others we're about,
taking care of down and out,
seeing friends as we should,
aiding others, doing good,
    lifting up those that fall,
giving comfort to one and all.
This is how it ought to be,
make it right, start with me.

Thank You Lord, now I see
many things in store for me.
Comfort zone out the door,
Lord for me you have much more.

Rutted is the operative word. So many times even though we care we let things slide on by. God wants us out of our area of comfort. We don't get excited if we're comfortable. We need excitement in our lives, both physically and spiritually. It gets the circulation going and makes us strong. Our health is important. Flabby Christianity is the pits.

For Granted

There are many things in this life
we take for granted every day,
the little things that are important,
though we don't treat them that way;
little ways we do things in living
our lives the way we choose,
to the bigger ones that come to us natural,
and we don't think about till we lose.
Take the washing of hands, for example,
or needing two hands for a load,
or supporting ourselves while reaching,
using paper at the bathroom commode.
Opening a jar can be stressful and taxing,
when it just won't go our way,
if we just have one hand for the using,
when we've used two till yesterday.
Taking the stairs on a run or slowly,
whatever the case may be,
is a gift from God to be cherished,
for we can lose it suddenly.
Even crutches can be a blessing or take,
for example, the wheelchair,
when our legs have been taken from us,
of other things we become aware.
Let us not take these things for granted,
that we are given to use each day;
just know that they come as blessings,
and let's be thankful in every way.

Psalm 50:1 "The mighty God, even the Lord, hath spoken, and called the earth from the rising of the sun unto the going down thereof."

The Shadow

What has caused the shadow that is in your life today?
Is it meant to guide you, or someone along your way?
Is it to protect you from something further on,
or is it meant to lift you up when it has passed along?

Sometimes there is a darkness, more than you want to bear,
with a weight upon your shoulders, others may not be aware.
Fears of the unknown grip you, when the light you do not see,
as you're passing through the tunnel of the shadow's agony.

Look beyond the shadow, you'll see God standing there
with his loving hand extended, when you've turned to
him in prayer.
He'll put his arms around you, and comfort you each time;
sometimes lifting you above it, to give you peace of mind.
He'll be there to assure you that he will give you rest,
and that he will go there with you, no matter what the test.
Lean on him completely, he'll smooth away the frown.
His answer is the right one, he'll never let you down.

Psalm 18:28 "For thou wilt light my candle: the Lord my God will enlighten my darkness."
Psalm 112:4 "Unto the upright there ariseth light in the darkness: he is gracious, and full of compassion, and righteous."

Isaiah 61:3

"To appoint unto them that mourn in Zion,
to give unto them beauty for ashes,
the oil of joy for mourning,
the garment of praise for the spirit of heaviness;
that they might be called trees of righteousness,
the planting of the Lord,
that he might be glorified."

God will never leave us alone. He has given us a free will
and it is of our choosing whether He is to abide with us or not.
We may be in a place where we cannot help ourselves, but
God did not put it upon us. Then is when it is prudent to be "prayed
up". He will provide someone to intercede for us.
We need to be on the listening end. God may want us to be
the intercessor. We may be God's extended hand at that moment.
Thank You Lord For Caring.

Depression

As depression sets upon me a big black hole is seen,
it completely surrounds me squeezing out the life that's been,
engulfed in total darkness not knowing where to turn,
not a light seen anywhere, not a candle there to burn.

It was as a tiny cloud seen upon the far horizon,
then completely over took me, blocking out the sun,
fog set in all around me, so thick it took my breath away,
who is there to help me, what has happened here today?

I stumble in the darkness, my steps are so unsure,
I falter without caring, everything is such a blur.
There is no one to help me, my friends seem to turn away,
they know not what I am facing, someone help me,
somehow, some way.

I feel that God's departed, it does not help to pray,
I'm in here alone, all by myself, someone show me a way.
God's not in the depression, of that I'm very sure,
or He would be here with me and would this awful dark deter.
Then it came unto my mind what I had to do,
I had to give praise unto the Lord in spite of what
I'm going through.

It raised up through the dark cloud, a pencil of light I see,
I keep on praising Jesus, now His love beams down on me.
It's cut a hole through the cloud, He's reaching down His hand,
His eyes of kindness pierce the fog, He does understand.

He was there all the time, just waiting for my okay
to intervene in my dark world, for His righteousness to display.
Thank You Lord for caring, for helping make this thing pass,
depression may overtake me, but with You it will not last.

Just A Touch

Just a touch was needed to relieve a fevered brow.
Just a touch was needed to bring a smile instead of "ow."
Just a touch was needed to smooth away a frown,
and keep the world around from going upside down.

A simple little gesture is sometimes all it takes
to help someone that's hurting to take away the aches
of something that has happened that we may not understand,
but let them know that we care by the touching of our hand.

Sometimes on is afraid to touch, or just don't realize
the good that is accomplished, or do not recognize
the fact that touching others was given us by God above,
from tiny infants on through life, to give of ourselves through love.

If you see someone that needs you, or you want to share your joy,
don't fear the gentle touching; done with care, it won't annoy.
Remember always when it's heartfelt, and we sincerely care that much,
life can be made for others easier, when we help with just a touch.

Matthew 14:36 "And besought him that they might only touch the hem of his garment: and as many as touched were made perfectly whole."

All it took was one little touch to be healed. That may be all it takes to calm and heal a broken heart or a bruised soul, just a touch of loving and caring. Reach out to others, as Christ has reached out to you.

Memories

There's a chest within the attic where many memories we do store,
mementos of the past, some way back from days of yore.
Included in the ancient chest is an old, old wedding dress
worn by a Grandmother once removed, one my daughters to impress.
There is the tiny dress worn in style by my Grandad
when he was a tiny boy, it was the nicest thing they had.
My son would be impressed with the suit Dad in the army wore
and my daughters would so like the dress of style my Mother
had when four.
The little boots that on my feet in winter time were worn,
would now by children of this time be laughed about and scorned.

The old family album holds many memories from over time,
grandparents, aunts and uncles, all the kids clear down to mine.
Then there is the old Bible with our family name by name,
births and deaths and weddings of all our kin we claim.
We find within the covers notes of joys and notes of grief,
but the ones that mean the most to me are the notes of the belief
of one that have passed from this life but left to us a treasure
of firm belief of our precious Lord; they were men of measure.

It is now upon my shoulders to pass this blessing on
to the ones that I love most, my daughters and my son.
A heritage far more precious than all the memories that are stored,
are the ones that have been left to us, an acquaintance with the Lord.

Thank You Lord for the memories designed within your divine plan,
may we forever have things to remember of you in our
families time span.

Proverbs 10:7a
"The memory of the just
is blessed."

God's Point of View

The day starts out the way it should in communion with the Lord,
I'm now having coffee with my friends talking about the world,
about many things that have happened, things that we would rue,
but are we seeing things the way we should from God's point of view?

We talk about the way we live our lives, of different things we know,
of different things we see and hear and places that we go.
We all have varied opinions of what we ought to do,
but I wonder if we take into account God's point of view?

We talk of things within the church, the changes that are being made,
are we following in God's footsteps or they prints that man has laid?
do we draw a line of right and wrong with things that to us are new,
are they coming from our perspective, or they God's point of view?

We need to pray and seek His face, to see if right is what we've heard.
We need to read the Bible, to study from His word.
We must take it all in context, not one verse, then let that do,
we must put it all together so we may see God's point of view.

We can never be too careful, we can't run with just anything,
we may make an error in judgement, disaster on ourselves to bring,
Let's not let ourselves be led astray, think before we say or do,
find out what God wants of us, what is God's point of view.

In this day and age we can never be too careful. Satan is going about as a roaring lion seeking whom he may devour. He is slipping little misleading tidbits into our lives any time he can. If we search the Word of God, taking everything just the way God had it written, we will find the answers to our questions. We may have to read more than we first intended, but it will do our hearts good. God will not let us down.

Attitude Adjustment

Woke up late this morning, couldn't get out of bed,
grumped and growled about the day, wanted to hold my head,
snapped rudely at my spouse, gave the children quite a fright,
no matter what was said, it was cause for another fight.
Knew I should read the Bible, a day like this I can't afford,
time for an attitude adjustment, "Praise the Lord!"

Things at work are hard today, people getting in the way,
contract isn't coming through, others around me have to pay.
Took the copy machine to task, broke a pencil or two,
made my partner feel bad, things I shouldn't do.
Have to face rest of the day, must work in one accord,
time for an attitude adjustment, "Praise the Lord!"

Made a fast trip to the grocery store, had to wait in line,
the one ahead seemed to dilly-dally taking time I felt was mine,
the cashier wasn't smiling, she snapped at all who passed,
I ground my teeth, growled a bit, hoped this wouldn't last.
Then the Lord spoke to me, His words with me have scored,
I needed an attitude adjustment, "Praise the Lord!"

When things take control of the head, actions get in the way
of a right relationship with people and with God, the devil
has his say.
Put him back into his place, quote to him the Word,
give to him the hard time, slay him with the Sword,
make him run for cover, you don't want his discord,
tell him you're getting an attitude adjustment, "Praise the Lord!"

If you think about it a little while, what do you own that is exclusively yours? You may say your house, car, life or health. But are they yours alone or are they just lent to you by God? Any of them can be taken from you at anytime without notice. Your words are the only thing that you, yourself, own. They are forever yours and can never be taken from you. Once they have come from your mouth they are yours. They may be sharp, soft, or just there but they are yours.

Proverbs 16:24 "Pleasant words are as an honeycomb, sweet to the soul and health to the bones."

My Words

Permanent, forever irrevocable
are the words I've said today,
as soon as they've gone from my mouth
they are in the air to stay.
They never can be taken back,
their trip is just one-way,
then they become elusive,
they are forever-and-away.
They are something that I own
eternally come what may,
for they were those said by me
and consequences are mine to pay.
Did I say ones to hurt others?
If I did, please Lord forgive,
for they never can be taken back,
they'll stay long as I live.
What other words might I have said,
did I give my children praise?
Those words are so important,
if they're mine they their spirits raise.
Were there words said by me in bitterness,
were they sharp unto my tongue,
did I say them all in kindness
or words that from wisdom sprung?
What other words belong to me?
For they open up my soul
to be scrutinized by others
like a large unending scroll.
Words are the only thing
that belong to me alone,
no one else can have them,
no one else can own.
They're on my permanent record,
may I take care in what I say,
for I don't want them to haunt me,
I'll be more careful starting today

1 Thessalonians 5:9-11a   "For God hath not appointed us to wrath, but to obtain salvation by our Lord Jesus Christ, who died for us, that, whether we wake or sleep, we should live together with him. Wherefore comfort yourselves together, and edify one another.

The Old Tee-Shirt

Tattered and worn the old tee-shirt that was thrown in the rag-bag today,
It's silent witness now gone forever from the streets where it had its say.
Worn with pride by someone
that used it as the sword
to all those who cared to read it,
a testimony for the Lord.
In this day of personal statements
worn by most to say how they think,
weird, outrageous, adventurous,
wanted to bring them to the brink
of social acceptance by those
who would be their peers,
trying to fill voids within them, to cover their doubts and fears.

This shirt, an eye catcher to others, making a statement of
peace and of love,
telling others about salvation paid for by Christ with his blood.
A few words of encouragement to an empty, hungry soul,
planting a seed of desire to be cleansed, to be made whole.

Yes, a silent witness of love, carried wherever we go
on the shirt now beyond wearing, God did bless it so.

We pray Lord, the one to follow will have meaning to others as well,
may it keep one of your children from mistakes that will send to hell.
Lord bless the wearer in their witness as they go along their way,
it's a tee-shirt but with your blessing they'll have a wonderful day.

Hospitality

As my brow is furrowed with thinking, things have come to me
about times in my younger life, things we now hardly see.
We often spent time with the neighbors, the whole family
together would go,
they in return would come see us, it became a natural flow.
The kids would play together, they always had lots of fun,
they used their imagination, they worked together as one.
The adults always had a good time with games and stories to tell,
homemade ice cream, popcorn and laughter blended with these so well.
We never seemed to get tired of each other, we enjoyed the company,
I miss these loved ones immensely, as they we no longer can see.

Times have changed in the passing, speed seems to prevail,
there's no time for each other, a friendship test I fear might fail.
Other things have become more important, the "boob tube"
fills the space,
running here or there takes priority, it's become a virtual "rat race."
Hospitality is a word in passing, friendship is "Hi there, let's go!"
Communication is for the telephone, with a portable we
march to and fro.
Would God be pleased with our reasons now that time is
moving so fast?
Let's take more time for each other, as we're all we have that will last.

*God's Word tells us in Romans 12:13 and 1 Peter 4:8 & 9
to love each other and offer hospitality to each other in God's
family. We don't know what we are missing when we don't have the
opportunity to spend time together. We need to forget about
keeping up with the Jones' and just be ourselves. That is the part
we want to get to know anyway. We need to slow down and relax in
each others company. God would surely bless us.*

Single Again

God has seen fit, in His infinite way,
to leave me alone again.
I don't understand why it's happened to me,
only God knows why my spouse, my friend.
Things weren't always what we wanted them to be,
but God knew how much we cared.
Our love to us was deep and strong,
and for this I was not really prepared.
The little things I thought were an irritant,
like the toothpaste cap, the paper or trash,
seems now to be so trivial,
I'd take them all back in a flash.
The little things I needed help with
I now have to do all alone;
I've found I must be much stronger
now that I'm on my own.
The things we shared together,
the laughter, the fun, the pain,
watching children, our friends, a snowstorm,
now the memories are all that remain.
There are times I feel I'm helpless
in facing this all alone,
but I know God gave friends to help me,
Lord please give me more backbone.
I pray Lord for strength and wisdom
as I travel down this lonesome road,
keep me sane and soothe the heartache,
thank You Lord for sharing my load.

2 Samuel 22:29 "For thou art my lamp, O Lord: and the Lord will lighten my darkness."

It seems that Sunday morning is the most hectic time of the week. That is the time that "Murphy's Law" takes effect. If anything can go wrong, it certainly will. But don't ever let that discourage you for God is still there. I think the Devil likes to see us squirm.

The question will come to mind, where is Dad? He's probably still reading the paper or trying to tie his tie. In most families I know Mom has taken the brunt of the action on Sunday morning. She's a survivor though.

Sunday Morning

Sweet little Johnnie Jump-up and cute little Suzzie Que,
are all dressed in their best bib-n-tucker ready for Sunday school.
Mom's checked ears all thoroughly, made sure to clean the face,
shoes are all tied securely, now Mom for herself must race.

The children take it upon themselves to go out to the car,
but other things catch their eyes, they don't get to far.
Johnnie steps on the toe of Suzzie's brand-new shoe,
scraping off the bright veneer making Suzzie blue.

She gives Johnnie such a shove, he lands face first on the ground,
scuffing nose, the knees and hands and makes an awful sound.
Mom comes running, she's all tied in knots, her primping has to wait,
for Johnnie and Suzzie are in a fight, Mom may be too late.
She grabs them both in frustration, their tail section she does warm,
she cleans them up as best she can, no one will see the harm.

She prays a prayer for guidance, heads them to the car once more,
gets them in one piece to the church just inside the door.
The welcoming committee asks how her day has been,
she says that things are really fine, her smile is a little thin.

She hears the choir in practice singing her favorite song,
it reaches out to her heart, turns all to right that's wrong.
She breathes a prayer in thanksgiving, for she knows now
that all is well,
God has met her this morning, she in His love can dwell.

When on your Sunday morning the Devil takes a hand,
Give all your cares to Jesus, He will understand.

Tomorrow's Yesterday

Day is moving fast, I'm getting far behind
I thought I had things really timed.
Miscalculation seems to have a way;
can't I put some off just one more day?

A brighter sun will on the morrow be,
things look better ahead for me.
Seems I said those things yesterday;
maybe that's the reason I now pay.

I'll sit to fool around a bit,
some magazine, or book will really hit,
then I can contemplate on what I'll do;
this was yesterday's scenario too.

Seems I've made myself a rut,
if I took just one day I'd catch up.
I need to see things differently,
then a happier person I would be.

Then the answer came to me,
it was so plain even I could see.
It put my priorities in fine array,
I'm already working tomorrow's yesterday.

James 4:13-15 "Go to now, ye that say, Today or tomorrow we will go into such a city, and continue there a year, and buy and sell, and get gain: whereas ye know not what shall be on the morrow. For what is your life? It is even a vapor, that appeareth for a little time, and then vanisheth away. For that ye ought to say, If the Lord will, we shall live, and do this, or that.

"No Fishing" Zone

Caught in the "NO FISHING" zone,
territory protected by God,
purchased by the blood of Christ on the cross,
off limits to his fishing rod.
He tried to sneak in anyway,
for he has many tricks up his sleeve,
bait and tackle well in hand,
not a thought in his mind to leave.
He baited and threw to you
the hook like he had the right,
temptation dangled in front of you,
it was something for you to delight.
A nibble would be so good,
a wrong thought and you would be had,
hooked in the jaw by the devils hand,
your demise would be so sad.
But you saw through his facade,
for you too, knew the rule,
you told him to get out, to leave,
that you wouldn't be played the fool.
You got him dead to rights,
his defenses had been blown,
there was nothing else for him to do,
for he's been caught in the "NO FISHING" zone.

You are protected by God,
a boundary has been set,
a hedge has been put all around you
when you with God have met.
Satan has lost out forever,
you have become God's own,
through God's word you are protected,
you've been placed in the "NO FISHING" zone.

Psalm 5:11 "But let all those that put their trust in thee rejoice: let them ever shout for joy, because thou defendest them: let them also that love thy name be joyful in thee."

Psalm 23

"The Lord is my shepherd; I shall not want.
He maketh me to lie down in green pastures:
he leadeth me beside the still waters.
He restoreth my soul:
he leadeth me in the paths of righteousness
for his name sake.
Yea, though I walk through the valley
of the shadow of death,
I will fear no evil: for thou art with me;
thy rod and thy staff they comfort me.
Thou preparest a table before me
in the presence of mine enemies:
thou anointest my head with oil;
my cup runneth over.
Surely goodness and mercy shall follow me
all the days of my life:
and I will dwell in the house of the Lord forever."

Alone

Alone, always alone, with masses of people everywhere,
ever in the crowd alone standing, needing someone to care.
Feeling rejected and lonely, bent head so no one would know,
the misery that I was feeling, as on their way they would go.

I was always the last one chosen when I was but a child,
growing up was a bitter experience to put it very mild.
No one cared if I existed, yet my heart was on my sleeve,
I cried for acceptance of others, it I did not receive.

One day I passed by a church door, a young person looked my way,
they smiled and said "Hi, come join us.", I couldn't turn away.
They sang of someone named Jesus, they prayed to the one
they called "Lord",
they talked together of comfort by someone that they adored.

For the first time I felt acceptance, warmth was everywhere,
love came to surround me, I wanted to stay there.
One came and told me of a Savior who had died on a cross for me,
he'd been rejected by others as I had, it was so I could be set free.

I prayed as that one suggested, I felt I was cleansed and made whole,
I never knew I'd been so important, that God had wanted my soul.

Now as I've grown much older, Jesus is a friend to me,
I've learned I can always trust him, although his face I can't see.
I am no longer lonely, I reach out to others instead,
for there are many that need my Jesus, I go where I am led.

Thank you Lord for that special someone who smiled at me that one day,
may I ever be so discerning, may I show someone the way
to your love and concern for their well-being like it was shown to me,
bless in this earthly endeavor, keep me true till your face I see.

My Friend Jesus

I'd heard tell that you loved me, I didn't know what to say,
no matter which way I turned, you seemed to be in my way.
People I knew said they knew you, that you were their best friend,
but I'd not made your acquaintance, I thought it would be a dead end.
They said you had made a sacrifice, that my life was the goal,
hearsay I don't give much thought to, I didn't want to be played the fool.

Advice of others passed right on by me, you beckoned, I turned away,
thoughts of self were the forefront, I thought I could keep you at bay.
Problems came in to surround me, some friends said you were the cause,
someone stepped in to defend you, I gave them no applause.

I could take it no longer, life seemed to take a nose dive,
the pit that I'd dug did surround me, I no longer thought I could survive.
You came to my side in the darkness, you reached out and took my hand,
you were gentle and kind beyond measure, how you knew I can't understand.
You lifted me out of my sorrow, you stood me again on firm ground,
your love seemed to completely surround me, the forgiveness
I needed I found.

You held nothing against me, you freed me from all my bonds,
my unconcern you freely forgave me, to my needs you did respond.
I don't know how I lived life without you, I'm sorry I waited so long,
I now must tell others about you, for you've fill my heart with song.

I sing of your love and completeness, I tell of my heart you healed,
I say with your blood you saved me, through your Word you are revealed.
Jesus you mean more than my life does, you've made me feel so clean,
I'm a new person now in Christ Jesus, now that you have come on the scene.

Thank You Lord for the trouble you went to so I could be whole,
now an eternal home in heaven is my daily earthly goal.
Bless those around that I contact, may they see you through me,
keep me and those I treasure till I see you in eternity.

*Matthew 11:28-30 "Come to me, all ye that labor and are
heavy laden, and I will give you rest. Take my yoke upon you, and
learn of me; for I am meek and lowly in heart:and ye shall find rest
unto your souls. For my yoke is easy, and my burden is light."*

Contentment

Contented, a hard thing to be, the world around prospers so,
"Why can't I do as they?" "Why can't I go where they go?"
Thoughts of greed given us by Satan, discontent his seed to sew,
greener grass across the fence, other's pastures do lure us so.

We live in the devil's playground, he sinned, we must pay,
for he makes for our lives misery if we let him have his way.
His time on this earth is short lived, God has said it would be,
don't let him distract us, for we have been made free.

We have treasures in heaven unending, don't let this earth come between
us and what is before us, when our savior's face is seen.
God does see what is needed for us in this life down here,
he has purpose if we let him lead us though our life without fear.

Don't give in to the discontentment Satan puts in our way,
for he is a snake of deepest deception, he's "getting his" some day.
Peace is a part of contentment, joy goes right along side,
goodness and love a blessing, when we in contentment abide.

Let's spend time reaching out to others, our minds on
God's work to stay,
then in contentment we'll be walking, self will have to give way.
Contentment is the right way, it is for us "real",
Satan get behind us, so God can our life fill.

2 Timothy 6:6-10 "But godliness with contentment is great gain. For we brought nothing into this world, and it is certain we can carry nothing out. And having food and raiment let us be therewith content. But they that will be rich fall into temptation and a snare, and into many foolish and hurtful lusts, which drown men in destruction and perdition. For the love of money is the root of all evil: which while some coveted after, they have erred from the faith, and pierced themselves through with many sorrows."

111

Real Treasure

We accumulate things of beauty, we want for ourselves more,
we lay away treasures of money, we keep hoards of stuff in store.
We sometimes don't share our blessings for they are ours alone,
we hang on to them for "dear life", they are parts of us that are shown.
They may become "tin god's" of our life style, things for others to see,
they may be amassed so we feel good, our security, though
misplaced it may be.

We let "things" dictate how we view things, they come between
us and God,
they hold away other people, for envy is in the path they have trod.
They shield us from the life of reality, for we hide behind things
that we own,
they make us feel we are better, our confidence becomes overblown.

Of this one thing I am certain, we will leave this earth all alone,
things of this earth won't matter when we face God on his throne.
Earthly security is gone forever, to the dust we will return,
our reward depends on Christ's shed blood, not what we try to earn.

There's only one thing we take with us, something worth more than gold,
that's souls that we've won to Christ Jesus by the
sharing of God's Word.

There is pleasure on earth for knowing we are doing what God has said,
but there is treasure in heaven unending for souls that to Christ are led.
Don't place stock in things that are earthly, for they shatter and decay,
place God first in your lifestyle, for other things he then makes the way.

Thank you God for your blessings as we with others share,
lead us in the way you want us, make us of yourself aware.

*Proverbs 11:28 "He that trusteth in his riches shall fall: but
the righteous shall flourish as a branch. vs. 30 The fruit of the
righteous is a tree of life; and he that winneth souls is wise."*
*Matthew 16:26a "For what is a man profited, if he shall
gain the whole world, and lose his own soul?"*

Family Reunion

"Hi there!" That's Aunt Maud, over there is Uncle Ed,
Cousin Josh is back behind them, where is Cousin Sid?
Aunt Elizabeth may be coming, Grandpa Jedadiah, too,
Sister Sue had to be here early, she waiting just for you.
Uncle Buck brought the twins, they're hard to tell apart,
Lulu came all by herself, bless her dear ole heart.
Henry came in on a plane, Mary rode the bus,
Jared brought his hotrod, Aunt Jo will make a fuss.
This year there are new babies, for last year two were wed,
so we can have a good time, seeing little ones are fed.
Jake is now a toddler, Mitch is all grown up,
Brenda is such a lady, she decided with us to sup.
We like to get together, to renew acquaintances again,
to introduce the youngsters to their other kin.
We fellowship together, eat and have some fun,
visit with each other, we become as one.

There is a great reunion we're preparing for someday soon,
we're going up to heaven with our Jesus to commune.
We'll see friends and loved ones, our great big family,
waiting now for us on earth to come, how happy we will be.
Our grandmas and our grandpas, aunts, uncles, cousins, too,
a little grandchild that didn't have a chance to see it's life here through,
are waiting there within the home that God prepared for us to be;
the banquet table now is set, come, go home with me.

Acts 10:2 "He and all his family were devout and God-fearing; he gave generously to those in need and prayed to God regularly."

I have a wonderful family heritage. We have a long line of God-fearing people. We are indeed blessed.

If you are not as fortunate, pray that God will start a revival in your families lives. Be patient and be ready, He may start with you. I want to see ALL my family in heaven. You included.

Ecclesiastes 9:11-12 "I have seen something else under the sun: The race is not to the swift or the battle to the strong, nor does food come to the wise or wealth to the brilliant or favor to the learned; but time and chance happen to them all. Moreover, no man knows when his hour will come: As fish are caught in a cruel net, or birds are taken in a snare, so men are trapped by evil times that fall unexpectedly upon them."

Proverbs 2:7-8 "He holds victory in store for the upright, he is a shield to those whose walk is blameless, for he guards the course of the just and protects the way of his faithful ones."

James 1:12   "Blessed is the man who perseveres under trial, because when he has stood the test, he will receive the crown of life that God has promised to those who love him."

1 John 2:25 "And this is what he promised us--even eternal life."

Christian Living

Every rose garden has it's thorns, amongst the wheat we find the tare,
weeds grow where the ground is fertile, though they were
not planted there.
Beauty is where we will see it, if that is what we're looking for;
encouraged hearts of the believer is given us by the Lord we adore.

We aren't promised an easy road when this life we elect to live,
unfairness is brought upon us, of natural origin it will pain to us give.

God's laws have been set in order, the just and the unjust receive,
sin overshadows this earthly existence even when we in God believe,
for we are living our life out in the area of Satan's domain;
it was given him by our creator just for awhile will he remain
as he is living on borrowed time since from heaven he fell,
then he will be cast with his demons into everlasting hell.

Many promises to us God has given, we find them all in his Word,
a home in heaven eternal, and comfort here in life is conferred.
He takes our hand through the rough trials, he gives light to
dark tunnels of need,
he carries us till we relinquish our burdens, he shields us so
Satan cannot succeed.
Love God with all of your heart, trust him through out your days,
know that he never will leave you, no matter what give him praise.

Your reward is not here but in heaven, continue to look up and ahead,
life down here is but a token, lean on what God's Word has said.
Life in the future is awesome, it's reality we really don't know,
just trust and believe for tomorrow when to life with our Savior we'll go.

Psalm 8:3-9   "When I consider thy heavens, the work of thy fingers, the moon and the stars, which thou hast ordained; what is man, that thou art mindful of him? and the son of man, that thou visited him? For thou hast made him a little lower than the angels, and hast crowned him with glory and honor.   Thou madest him to have dominion over the works of thy hands; thou hast put all things under his feet: All sheep and oxen, yea, and all the beasts of the field; the fowl of the air, and the fish of the sea, and whatsoever passeth through the paths of the seas. O Lord our Lord, how excellent is thy name in all the earth!"

Praise God

The song in the stream as it moves along
over rocks and rills on the way
to the destination where it meets the sea,
ne're from it's banks to stray.
The music sent forth by the leaves of the trees
as they sing to us in the eve,
as the breezes pass, rustling them in fun,
when through the trees it does weave.
The bull frog croaking from the bank
of a lake on a summer's night,
while locust and crickets join in crooning a tune
made for us to delight.
The light of the stars twinkle so bright
in the clear, open sky we see,
making for us a world all our own
rivaled by none other that be.

The praise in our hearts rise to match
the ones that so closely surround
us at this time of reverent joy
that only through God's love can be found.
Rejoice, rejoice in what God has done,
his creation is for us to enjoy,
let us rest in knowledge of what he can do,
let his blessings our sorrows destroy,
for we see in this sky and hear these sounds
to wash away all fear
of what it would take from our hearts at this time,
what we hold so dear.
Peace, sweet peace, a love for life,
warmth of family and friends,
enclosed in a life we know every day,
in which God through his love blends.

Rest and know that God is good,
he will be with us to face another day,
he just lets us know he is here for us
in a wonderful, marvelous way.

Genesis 8:22 "While the earth remaineth, seedtime and harvest, and cold and heat, and summer and winter, and day and night shall not cease."

Ecclesiastes 3:1-2 "To every thing there is a season, and a time to every purpose under the heaven: a time to be born, and a time to die; a time to plant, and a time to pluck up that which is planted."

Galatians 6:7-9 "Do not be deceived; God is not mocked: for whatsoever a man soweth, that shall he also reap. For he that soweth to his flesh shall of the flesh reap corruption; but he that soweth to the Spirit shall of the Spirit reap life everlasting. And let us not be weary in well doing: for in due season we shall reap, if we faint not."

John 4:35-37 "Say not ye, There are yet four months, and then cometh harvest? Behold, I say unto you, Lift up your eyes, and look on the fields; for they are white already to harvest. And he that reapeth receiveth wages, and gathereth fruit unto life eternal: that both he that soweth and he that reapeth may rejoice together. And herein is that saying true, One soweth, and another reapeth."

The Harvest

Large stacks of pretty bales dot the country side around,
while the smell of new mown hay fills the air.
Combines lined up side by side progressing through the field,
as golden wheat gives up it's heads with a flair.

Later on as fall arrives other crops their produce give,
filling grain bins and lofty silos with their yield,
while the gardens 'round about, filled with tasty treats,
are preserved and at a later date revealed.

A greater harvest yet before us ready lays,
souls in numbers waiting for our lives to touch.
Planted near within the circle of our lives from day to day,
so that God, through us, can love them very much.

We can lead them ever gently to the knowledge of God's love,
by our actions and our words along the way,
being ever mindful that the things they hear and see,
are the message that within their heart will stay.

The time for us to harvest may be very short indeed,
as we are waiting even now for God's return.
Let us ever ready be, living life the way we should,
so that others through our lives for God will yearn.

My Mother's Love

My Mother's love I count on,
I know that she'll be there
to lend me her listening ear,
to help me when I share
with moral support, or guiding hand,
or kneel with me in prayer.
My burden will be much lighter
when I have Mother to care.

Sometimes I give her quite a start,
other times she can not tell
that I have been listening
to the advice she gives so well.
Maybe it's not what I want to hear
and it sometimes will take time;
I know when before the Lord she goes
things will turn out fine.

There are many fine Mothers around,
God didn't make one and rest,
but of this one thing I am certain:
he made my Mother the best.

You may wonder why I left this poem for this spot.
If you've read this far, you will see what I believe and what
I have become because of my parent's influence. Yes, I had to
choose for myself, but it is important to be raised the right way so
that the choices for right are bold and bright in the forefront.
Thank God for good parents.

That's
Life

The Museum

We went to a museum, many antiques we did see,
wood stoves, ice boxes, wash boards, oh you, oh my, oh me.

They talked about sod houses, hand pumps, out-houses too,
we stood by hitching posts and heard what blacksmiths had to do.

Descriptions were of traveling along the Oregon trail,
how horses went from place to place delivering all the mail.

The railroad came into being, more settlements were made,
as they set up many brand-new towns giving place for all to trade.

Many nationalities came and settled, each to their own space,
so there was common understanding of their own speech and race.

They brought from the "old country" a number of different skills,
needed in this new frontier that lacked the modern frills.

They learned to live together, to respect each others needs,
created new horizons, as westward they did speed.

They found that in each other were many a varied trait,
that bound them close together as they begin to integrate.

Now we're all American's, differences are hard to see,
for we've created our own world where you are one with me.

Things have changed an awful lot in the recent past,
our new modern technology now a new frontier has cast.

My mind has formed a question as all these antiques we did see,
I've seen many used in and around our home, so what does
that make me?

*Reminders of our past can be a pleasant experience. Teaching
our younger ones is fun. We realize the great changes that have been
made in our lifetime. God has been very good to us.*

Country Livin'

Country life, to everyone, is a choice that's not been given.
It was born with me, a wondrous life, this gift of country livin'.
I've had a taste of city life as I thought I'd give a try,
but the country blood within my veins laid down and tried to die.

The city seemed to try and take from me God given freedom,
for it boxed me in, closed me off from the space I'd had to live in.
My horse I'd had to leave at home, my dog did have to stay,
as the apartment wasn't big enough and wouldn't get that way.

It seemed that buildings were in the way, closing
access to the heavens,
and the neighborhood, though friendly, was too close
for me to be in.
The animal varieties were just caged birds, small dogs, or cats,
even country sized mosquitoes had shrunk to pesky gnats.

There were always people noises, every hour night or day,
masking natures soothing lullabies, nerve endings to decay.

Golden grain on the horizon, fresh mowed hay smells in the air,
the rooster crowing at day's dawning, left me longing to be there.

I packed my bags and moved back to the place that I belong,
giving God the glory, and told Him I'd been so wrong.
If I get a yen for city life again I'll go for just the day,
for I'm addicted to country livin' and will always be that way.

Fishin'

Top of the mornin' to you, greetings to one and all.
Had an undisturbed night of sleeping, fresh air and starlight did lull.
My tackle is ready and waiting, the worms will not a bird meet,
for fish are on my agenda, this day will be so sweet.
Fish, be hungry and waiting, my bait I hope will entice,
a bite is all that is needed for you to be caught on my device.
Bend my rod as you fight to escape me, put up a fight and try to run,
get away, if you can, with your breakfast, for me this will be much fun.

Exercise like this is needed to make my "kinks" unwind,
a time to relax in the sunlight, a time to clear my mind.
Joy in the day is before me, luxury of ease is ahead,
this is a time of refreshing, a time when life's burdens are shed.
Peace and relaxation is wanted, laughter and cheer my delight,
being here to play at fishin' is what I will keep in my sight.
This is to make me a memory, something to hold to the rest of the year,
to dwell on when things close around me, a pause to make things clear.

God gave us these things to rest us, to each and everyone his own.
Thank you Lord for this blessing, to me again you have yourself shown.

The Giant

There's a giant on the corner standing all alone,
keeping sentry duty longer than neighbors have been born.
Silent but ever watching as the years have come and gone,
seeing all the changes that more than a century did spawn.

There was the horse and buggy, the big old wagon, too,
they gave way to the horseless carriage, oh they will of this day rue.
But the cars have taken over, big trucks came into view,
to say the least about the school bus, it's a real lulu.
There is a strange two-wheeled vehicle, a bicycle it is called,
is still around but some have changed when a motor was installed.
It's called a motorcycle but just two wheels can still be seen,
it goes every bit as fast as the cars, they sound like they are mean.

Mud roads close by were graveled, now some are paved or "oiled,"
the neighbor hood has changed a bit, but nothing has been spoiled.

The giant on the corner spreads it's protecting arms,
shading all that come it's way from the warm rays of the sun.
Though many storms have taken toll, the great cottonwood still stands,
to fulfill its God-given duty, what its stately life demands.
It's twisted some and has lost branches too, for life is ne'er the same,
but it won't give up, till that last big storm calls the last refrain.
Then it'll fall with grace in one big crash, this giant forever gone,
to join memories of things that's past; our life will continue on.

Coffee Toper

"Coffee toper? What's that?" you say.
It's one who starts at break of day
with cup in hand all day long,
until at last the day is done.

"I'm not addicted." you'll hear him say,
but the cup in hand speaks the other way.
The nerves are shot, the head does ache
unless the coffee is there to take.

"Try caffeine free," is the offer made,
but without real stuff the head will fade.
"No cream, or sugar, just black and strong,"
that's what you hear in the toper's song.

In cup or mug, thermos, or pot,
there's no difference made to the coffee sot.

But it's well known, both far and wide,
that the toper doesn't have to hide,
for they're not a menace to someone else,
just hard on no one, but themselves.

Another truth we can't evade,
over coffee cups, fast friends are made.
So no matter what else we say,
a coffee toper is just okay!

Grandpa's Teeth!

He was always rather common,
he lived quite modestly.
He never climbed the highest mount,
he never went to sea.

But he made a strong impression
at little Stevie's house
the day he left the dentist shop
with gold caps in his mouth.

His guns and cars and saddle horse
the other kids could own;
Steve said, "I want those golden teeth
when you are dead and gone."

So Grandpa fixed it in his will
so everyone would know
that Stevie got his bright gold caps
when Grandpa had to go.

Now since he's gone up Glory road,
that luscious fruit to eat;
the old boy has to gum it
cause Stevie's got his teeth.

Keith Blauvelt

This is the day that God made for you.

Be happy!

God Bless!

LaDean   McGonigle

Table Of Contents

Sections:

Contents By Sections:

Friendship & Love:

Children & Families:

That's Life:

To order additional copies of **Quiet Waters Of Inspiration,** complete the information below.

Ship to: (please print)

Name _____

Address _____

City, State, Zip _____

____Copies of **Quiet Waters Of Inspiration** @ $9.95 ea. $_____

Postage and handling @ $2.75 per book $_____

Nebraska residents add 5% tax $_____

Total amount enclosed $_____

Make checks payable to **Quiet Waters Of Inspiration**

**Send to: LaDean McGonigle, P.O. Box 24
Beaver Crossing, NE 68313-0024**

....

To order additional copies of **Quiet Waters Of Inspiration,** complete the information below.

Ship to: (please print)

Name _____

Address _____

City, State, Zip _____

____Copies of **Quiet Waters Of Inspiration** @ $9.95 ea. $_____

Postage and handling @ $2.75 per book $_____

Nebraska residents add 5% tax $_____

Total amount enclosed $_____

Make checks payable to **Quiet Waters Of Inspiration**

**Send to: LaDean McGonigle, P.O. Box 24
Beaver Crossing, NE 68313-0024**